Multi Method Supply Planning in SAP APO

Shaun Snapp

Multi Method Supply Planning in SAP APO

For information about this title or to order other books and/or electronic media, contact the publisher:
SCM Focus Press
PO Box 29502 #9059
Las Vegas, NV 89126-9502
http://www.scmfocus.com/scmfocuspress
(408) 657-0249

ISBN: 978-1-939731-03-6

Printed in the United States of America

Cover and interior design by: 1106 Design

Contents

CHAPTER 1

Introduction

The motivation for this book was quite simple. A great deal is written on why some supply planning methods are better than others. But, while working on a mixed supply planning method approach for a client, I could find no books or articles on the topic of how to successfully integrate multiple methods into an advanced planning implementation or even within an ERP system. I was surprised by this finding and realized that many companies out there must be curious about how to make multiple supply planning methods work together in either one or multiple software applications. Therefore, this book addresses what I view as a gap in the published information on the use and configuration of mixed supply planning methods.

When I reviewed my planning implementation projects going back to 1997, I realized that many companies must have had the business requirement to be able to use multiple methods. Furthermore, many companies must have been dissuaded from using multiple methods (at least within a single system), probably as a "bleed-over" from the sales process. In fact, it can be surprising—or shocking depending upon your perspective—how much the implementation of software can be guided—and in many cases misguided—by constructs used during the sales process, a perfect example of this being "best practices." A best practice is a concept that does not hold up under scrutiny once evaluated (as is discussed in the following article).

http://www.scmfocus.com/sapprojectmanagement/2010/07/how-valid-are-saps-best-practice-claims/

Statements made during the sales process have no theoretical boundary; as nothing is actually done during the sales process, there is no need to keep to reality. In fact, reality-based selling is a disadvantage during the sales process and considered a sign of "small thinking." After many years working in the enterprise software market, I have learned never to underestimate the lies told by enterprise software salesmen.

There was once a Vice President of Sales at a company I worked with. During a sales meeting, he gave a presentation in which he described new products that were pipe dreams at that point in time. Part way through the presentation, one salesman raised his hand and said:

"That is nice Greg, but the things you are talking about are like two to three years away."

The Vice President of Sales responded: "I never want to hear the fact that something does not exist as an excuse to not sell."

More about the advantages of lying in the enterprise software market are discussed in the following article:

http://www.scmfocus.com/enterprisesoftwarepolicy/2012/03/08/how-lying-is-an-advantage-in-the-enterprise-software-market/

As an independent consultant, I can afford to lampoon the sales process. However, senior representatives and even the consulting arms of the vendors (i.e., those doing the work on projects) cannot, as they are required to perpetuate the message delivered during the sales process. If you and I could speak privately for a moment, without the brash intrusion of a software salesperson or some hyper-aggressive partner at a major consulting firm, I would say that the truth is there is no one right supply planning method for all situations, even within one company.

This book brings forward a specific perspective that is simply not discussed very often. The philosophy proposed by this book—a philosophy that did not come from academic papers or books, but instead was derived holistically from working on many supply planning projects over a number of years—is as follows:

> *"It is unnecessary to choose a single supply planning method. Mixing various supply planning methods is both feasible and will, in almost all situations, add more value over using a single method."*

While debates on various methods often emphasize one method over another, in actuality, each method has some advantages and some disadvantages. There is no single supply planning method that meets all requirements within a company. Part of the book is dedicated to explaining why this is the case, and another part of the book is dedicated to showing the results of testing, which demonstrate quite clearly that multiple methods can be effectively combined to make a coherent supply plan.

SAP SNP versus Other Supply Planning Applications

This book focuses on SAP SNP, one of the most popular supply planning applications. In doing so, I am not endorsing the application. SAP SNP just happens to be an application for which I provide consulting services, and therefore, I have access to and experience in configuring and adjusting the application. The lessons learned can be applied to other supply planning applications, but of course the specific settings that are covered here would not apply. Exactly how the settings must be changed, and how the vendor has designed their application to work with different supply planning methods, would have to be evaluated on a vendor-by-vendor basis. SAP SNP is the most complex and difficult-to-configure application in supply planning. If I am able to demonstrate how to configure SNP to support multiple supply planning methods, accomplishing the same objective in easier-to-use software should be a smaller feat. However, the concept of using mixed supply planning methods applies to all vendors.

The Use of Screen Shots in the Book

I consult in some popular and well-known applications, and I've found that companies have often been given the wrong impression of an application's capabilities. As part of my consulting work, I am required to present the results of testing and research about various applications. The research may show that a well-known application is not able to perform some functionality well enough to be used by a company, and point to a lesser-known application where this functionality is easily performed. Because I am routinely in this situation, I am asked to provide evidence of the testing results within applications, and screen shots provide this necessary evidence.

Furthermore, some time ago it became a habit for me to include extensive screen shots in most of my project documentation. A screen shot does not, of course, guarantee that a particular functionality works, but it is the best that can be done in a document format. Everything in this book exists in one application or another, and nothing described in this book is hypothetical.

How Writing Bias is Controlled at SCM Focus and SCM Focus Press

Bias is a serious problem in the enterprise software field. Large vendors receive uncritical coverage of their products, and large consulting companies recommend the large vendors that have the resources to hire and pay consultants rather than the vendors with the best software for the client's needs.

Just as in my consulting practice, I do not financially benefit from a company's decision to buy an application that I showcase in print, either in a book or on the website. SCM Focus has the most stringent rules related to controlling bias and restricting commercial influence of any information provider. These "writing rules" are provided in the link below:

http://www.scmfocus.com/writing-rules/

If other information providers followed these rules, I would be able to learn about software without being required to perform my own research and testing for every topic.

Information about enterprise supply chain planning software can be found on the Internet, but this information is primarily promotional or written at such a high level that none of the important details or limitations of the application are exposed; this is true of books as well. When only one enterprise software application is covered in a book, one will find that the application works perfectly; the application operates as expected and there are no problems during the implementation to bring the application live. This is all quite amazing and quite different from my experience of implementing enterprise software. However, it is very difficult to make a living by providing objective information about enterprise supply chain software, especially as it means being critical at some point. I once remarked to a friend that SCM Focus had very little competition in providing untarnished information on this software category, and he said, "Of course, there is no money in it."

The Approach to the Book

By writing this book, I wanted to help people get exactly the information they need without having to read a lengthy volume. The approach to the book is essentially the same as to my previous book, *Inventory Optimization and Multi Echelon Planning Software,* and in writing this book, I followed the same principles.

1. **Be direct and concise.** There is very little theory in this book and the math that I cover is simple. A number of books cover supply planning mathematics and I did not want to repeat something that has already been covered extensively in other sources or in my other books. As is stated several times in this book, for a full explanation of the different supply planning methods, please see my book, *Supply Planning with MRP, DRP and APS Software.*

2. **Based on project experience.** Nothing in the book is hypothetical; I have worked with it or tested it on an actual project. My project experience has led to my understanding a number of things that are not covered in typical supply planning books. In this book, I pass on this understanding to you.

3. **Saturate the book with graphics.** Roughly two-thirds of a human's sensory input is visual, and books that do not use graphics—especially educational and training books such as this one—can fall short of their purpose. Graphics have also been used consistently and extensively on the SCM Focus website.

Before writing this book, I spent some time reviewing what has already been published on the subject. This book is different from other books in terms of its intended audience and its scope. It is directed toward people that have either worked with ERP or know what it is; I am assuming that the reader has a basic knowledge level in this area. While it concentrates on supply planning, rather than focusing on any one particular supply planning method, this book covers all of the supply planning methods (with the exclusion of inventory optimization and multi-echelon, for which I have written a separate book).

The Book's Roadmap
Some of the feedback during the review stage of the book was that because the topic is complex, the reader could benefit from a roadmap that lays out where the book is going to go. In that spirit, I have included the graphic on the following page:

Book Roadmap

Chapter Category	Background Chapters	Testing Chapters	Implementation Chapters
Purpose	*A Conceptual Introduction to the Multi Method Approach*	*How the the Multi Method Approach Behaves*	*Multi Method Approach Practical Implementation Issues*
Chapters/Topics	CH 1. Introduction	CH 4. Preparing the Prototype for Multi Method Testing	CH 6. Coding the Product Location Database/Spreadsheet
	CH 2. The Different Supply Planning Methods Available within SAP SNP	CH 5. Prototyping the Multi Method Supply Planning Model	CH 7. Planning Beyond a Single Method per Echelon
	CH 3. Combining Supply Methods Across External Planning Systems and ERP Systems		CH 8. Creating a Dynamic Selection for Automatic Product Location Switching Between Methods
			CH 9. Overcoming the Human and Information Challenges of the Multi Method Approach
			CH 10. Combining SNP with Inventory Optimization and Multi Echelon Planning

The SCM Focus Site

As I am also the author of the SCM Focus site, http://www.scmfocus.com. The site and the book share a number of concepts and graphics. Furthermore, this book contains many links to articles on the site, which provide more detail on specific subjects. This book provides an explanation of how supply planning software works and aims to continue to be a reference after its initial reading. However, if your interest in supply planning software continues to grow, the SCM Focus site is a good resource to which articles are continually added.

The SCM site dedicated specifically to supply planning is http://www.scmfocus.com/supplyplanning.

The site dedicated to SAP planning is http://www.scmfocus.com/sapplanning

Intended Audience

The feedback I received from early reviewers described this book as good for any person who wants to understand exactly how to flexibly and completely combine supply planning methods, as well as to see a proof of concept of how this would work in SAP APO. If you have any questions or comments on the book, please e-mail me at shaunsnapp@scmfocus.com.

Abbreviations

A listing of all abbreviations used throughout the book is provided at the end of the book.

CHAPTER 2

The Different Supply Planning Methods Available within SAP SNP

One of the most important things to do on an APO project, or on any supply chain planning project, is to cover the different supply planning methods which are available in APO, secondly how they relate to one another, and thirdly how they relate to the business requirements. This graphic on the following page helps to delineate the methods and sub methods available within SAP SNP.

Product Location Combination		Advanced Methods		Heuristic					
Product	Location	CTM	Optimizer	Heuristic With No Modifier	Reorder Point (Forward Calc)	Reorder Point (Non-Forward Calc) - Customized	Target Days Supply	Target Stock Levels
123	San Diego	X						
123	San Francisco				X			
123	Los Angeles			X				
123	San Jose					X		
567	San Diego	X						
657	San Francisco							X
Characteristics of Each Method								
Uses a Forecast?		Yes	Yes	Yes	No	Yes	Yes	No
Product is Forecastable?		Yes	Yes	Yes	No	Yes	Yes	No
Constrained Method?		Yes	Yes	No	No	No	No	No

[1]One method of supply planning that is left out of the graphic above is inventory optimization and multi echelon planning (MEIO). This method does not exist in SNP. I discuss the integration of an external MEIO application with SNP in Chapter 5: "Prototyping the Multi-Method Supply Planning Model." MRP or DRP are also not included, as these two methods do not exist in SNP and are the standard supply planning methods available in SAP ERP. For both, the SNP heuristic and the deployment heuristic are more sophisticated alternatives. I should also note that these options are for the initial supply plan. DRP (as was as the deployment heuristic) are part of the deployment plan, which follows the initial supply plan. I will discuss the different methods in more detail in Chapter 3: "Combining Supply Planning Methods Across External Planning Systems and ERP Systems."

Terminology such as reorder points and target stock levels (which I refer to as "planning modifiers") are sometimes used interchangeably with the term "method" or are sometimes called a master data parameter, and each significantly controls the planning output.

However, in SNP a reorder point, target stock level, or target days do not work by themselves. They are modifiers and run in conjunction with the SNP heuristic. The SNP heuristic

---

[1] Because I have written an entire book on the different supply planning methods *(Supply Planning with MRP, DRP and APS Software)*, I will not touch on how the individual methods work. This book will instead focus on how to how to use the methods together.

can be run without any modification, as per the option, "Heuristic With No Modification," listed in the previous graphic. All of the modifiers are listed underneath the "Heuristic" heading. The term "modifier" is not a standardized term; however, it is quite appropriate for describing the interaction between these specific master data parameters (which are all located on the lot size tab of the product location master in SNP).

A matrix of this type can be used to code all product locations (a few examples which I have coded in the graphic above) for the entire product database.

The supply planning methods are selected during configuration, which is covered in Chapter 5: "Prototyping the Multi Method Supply Planning Model." However, the method modifications are set in the Lot Size tabs of the Product-Location Master. How to assign different "master data parameters" or modifiers to different product locations is very well known. A central concept of this book is that both method modifiers as well as the actual method can be assigned per product location.

Decoding the Statements Regarding the Supply Planning Methods Used

Often, the primary method being used to plan the supply network will be used to generalize over all of the product locations that are included in the implementation. For instance, when you ask a person working on a supply planning implementation what is being implemented, he or she will often say something like, "We are using optimization, or a heuristic," describing the major method that is being used to plan the supply network. This statement can mean several things. In rare circumstances, the statement can be taken literally to mean that all of the product-location combinations in the supply network are planned by the method quoted. However, in many cases it means that some product-location combinations are planned with the method named and some product-location combinations are planned with another method. This can be accomplished inside one system (for instance in SAP APO) or in two systems (in SAP APO and SAP ERP). The graphic on the following page describes some of the important common implications for using a single or multiple supply planning method approach across one versus two systems.

Options	Solution Considerations		Implementation Considerations	
	Complexity	Number of Supply Planning Applications	Required Planner Training	Hardware Requirements in APO
All Product Locations are planned with one supply planning method.	Low	1	Avrerage	High
Some product locations are planned with one supply planning method and others with another method.	High	1	Average	High
Some product locations are planned with one method in ERP and other product locations are planned with another method in APO.	Medium	2	High	Average

The Methods Available for Supply Planning

Before we get into how to use multiple supply planning methods, let's review the supply planning methods that are available. Now is also a good time to explain that this book covers multiple methods for either the S&OP and rough-cut capacity plan or the initial supply plan, but does not cover using multiple methods for the deployment plan or for the redeployment. There is a reason for this: while S&OP, rough-cut capacity plan and the initial supply plan use the same methods, only in rare instances would the deployment and redeployment plan use multiple methods. A brief explanation of the different supply planning threads is included below:

1. S&OP & Rough-Cut Capacity Plan: These long range planning threads are generally not part of the live environment. They are used for analytical purposes rather than to drive recommendations to the ERP system.

2. The Initial Supply Plan (performed by MRP in ERP systems): Produces initial production and procurement plan. Is focused on bringing stock into

the supply network, and in creating stock with planned production orders. Can also be called the master production schedule (MPS), if the initial supply plan is run under certain criteria.

http://www.scmfocus.com/supplyplanning/2011/10/02/the-four-factors-that-make-up-the-master-production-schedule/

3. The Deployment Plan (performed by DRP in ERP systems): Focused on pushing stock from locations at the beginning of the supply network to the end of the supply network.

4. The Redeployment Plan (performed by specialized applications with redeployment functionality or with a custom report): Focused on repositioning stock, which is already in the supply network to locations where it has a higher probability of consumption.

http://www.scmfocus.com/inventoryoptimizationmultiechelon/2011/10/redeployment/

The Complexity of Method Combination

The tricky part is in understanding how to logically combine the different methods into a coherent solution. Much time is spent debating among the different supply planning methods, but very little is written on how to properly integrate multiple methods. That is unfortunate because all methods and method modifiers can be of value in some circumstances. Furthermore, the various supply planning methods cannot not be compared simply on the basis of their sophistication, the most common way to grade each method. Some methods are extremely sophisticated, but are also complex, expensive and challenging to implement, to troubleshoot and to explain. For instance, the most complex methods in supply planning are optimization (both cost based and inventory optimization and multi echelon planning). These methods can provide superior output if implemented correctly, but they cost quite a bit more to implement.

There are debates as to which methods have the highest maintenance costs, because maintenance must be segmented into the costs associated with the planners (or the business side of maintenance) versus the IT costs of maintaining the solution. For example, most companies that implemented advanced supply planning applications since the mid-1990s are, in fact, still using MRP and DRP. While these applications are inexpensive to maintain from an IT perspective (relatively speaking), they require more maintenance by planners who must make adjustments to the results.

Because this topic is complex and multifaceted, I will halt the coverage here. It is, however, a primary topic of my book, *Supply Planning with MRP, DRP and APS Software.* A complex supply planning method may be a perfect fit for a company; the company may implement it quite well. However, a complex supply planning method may take too much processing time for every product location in the entire supply network, but moving some product locations that do not require the complexity of the solution to a simpler method may reduce the run time of the planning run, making the overall solution feasible.

Frequently the decision of which method to use is made without truly understanding the costs and benefits of different methods. For instance, the following limitations apply to method selection:

1. Many companies are driven to constraint-based approaches, but may lack the interest or dedication to maintain the resource constraint master data. Companies that implement constraint-based planning generally must increase their investment in master data and their ability to maintain master data. Most companies are willing to purchase new software, but the investment required to build up a company's master data capabilities is a much tougher sell.

2. Supply planning applications are sold on the basis of being able to plan on multiple types of capacity constraints. In actual practice, the vast majority of companies that do perform constraint-based planning only constrain on production resources. Therefore, most of the code for other types of resources goes unused. More on resources can be found at the following link:

   http://www.scmfocus.com/sapplanning/2008/09/14/resources/

3. Companies often select CTM because they want to be able to prioritize either demand or supply or both. However, without a clear plan for how to

make these decisions, companies can end up implementing CTM without performing very much prioritization at all.

http://www.scmfocus.com/sapplanning/2009/12/08/customer-prioritization-and-ctm/

4. Companies may select cost optimization, but without putting any effort into determining if they can actually set the costs that are necessary to drive the optimizer properly. Companies can go on for years without even evaluating the costs, or just as bad, with an IT department which attempts to protect or hide the flaws in the cost design as well as the overall configuration from the business in order to maintain the system's "credibility."

Arriving at the right combination of supply planning methods requires a detailed study of all the requirements and data necessary to drive the method. Without that upfront effort and knowledge, a method can end up being selected, and then simply be perpetuated because of the strong tendency not to change decisions after they have been made.

To return to the selection of methods and method modifiers, the graphic shown previously is provided again below:

Product Location Combination		Advanced Methods		Heuristic				
Product	Location	CTM	Optimizer	Heuristic With No Modifier	Reorder Point (Forward Calc)	Reorder Point (Non-Forward Calc) - Customized	Target Days Supply	Target Stock Levels
123	San Diego	X						
123	San Francisco				X			
123	Los Angeles			X				
123	San Jose					X		
567	San Diego	X						
657	San Francisco							X
Characteristics of Each Method								
Uses a Forecast?		Yes	Yes	Yes	No	Yes	Yes	No
Product is Forecastable?		Yes	Yes	Yes	No	Yes	Yes	No
Constrained Method?		Yes	Yes	No	No	No	No	No

The method modifiers controlled at the product location master. These settings are shown in the screenshots on the following page.

The Lot Size tab of the Product-Location Master has two sub-tabs. These two sub-tabs contain the method modifiers. SAP SNP has an enormous number of fields on its product-location master. In contrast, Demand Works Smoothie has a single "tab" for all of the supply planning parameters.

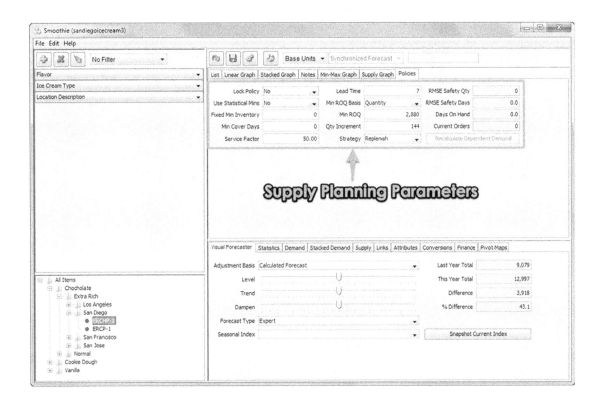

The method modifiers that can be configured on these tabs are:

1. Reorder Point
2. Target Stock Level
3. Target Days' Supply
4. Maximum Stock Level
5. Lot Size (units)
6. Lot Size (periodic)

How the methods and moderating controls interact with the three major methods can be seen in the graphic below:

Reorder Point, TSL, TDS, Max Stock Level, and Lot Size and Major Supply Planning Methods						
(Major) Planning Method	Reorder Point	Target Stock Level	Target Days Supply	Maximum Stock Level	Lot Size (Units)	Period Lot Size
SNP Heuristic	X	X	X	X	X	X
Capable to Match						
SNP Optimizer				X	X	

The first thing to understand is that not all SNP methods work with all of the method modifiers. For instance, in SNP, reorder points can be used with the SNP Heuristic, but cannot be used with either the SNP optimizer or CTM. The target stock level can be used with the SNP optimizer, but not with CTM. Therefore, both the reorder point and the target stock level are heuristic-based planning modifiers. Essentially, most of these methods interoperate with the SNP heuristic, but for the most part do not work with CTM or the optimizer. While one may ask, "Why not?" there is logic to this combination of methods and method modifiers. There could be a point where applying a method modifier to some methods would tend to interfere with the method's overriding objective.

In the past, companies have been locked into the options that are available for their method. However, using the approach outlined in this book, a company can literally have almost any combination of the alternatives listed on the previous page. (Any combination with the possible caveat: A company may not be willing to pay for the implementation of two complex methods—such as CTM and the optimizer—in a single implementation. I say "possible" caveat because I have seen companies implement both a cost optimizer and an inventory optimization application, so I need to be careful before applying very hard and fast rules.)

Why Are There Two Reorder Point Modifiers?

One item from the graphic that should be explained is why there are two reorder points to choose from. The two options are not related to what the reorder point uses for its determination, or the alternatives presented in the product-location master, but whether it forward calculates or does not forward calculate beyond the replenishment lead time—that is how far out into the future the reorder point looks forward in time. The following phrase is repeated in any number of books on inventory management and supply planning, in some shape or form:

"Reorder points are a non forecast-based method for supply planning."

However, while a reorder point does not require a forecast, in SAP ERP it will use forecast-driven requirements to calculate a reorder point—out to the point of replenishment lead time. And the story changes once again, once we begin to discuss reorder points in SAP APO. So there are some shades of grey related to whether and how much reorder points are dependent upon a forecast, which is system dependent.

However, SAP APO SNP changed the calculation method so that it calculates forward beyond the replenishment lead time. In SAP APO, as long as forecasts are entered, and because the reorder points in APO calculate on the basis of planned stock on hand (and not actual stock on hand), reorder point-based orders can be created for the entire planning horizon. SAP has converted the reorder point to be a forecast-based planning method. The following mockup of the SAP APO planning book (the main user interface for SAP DP and SAP SNP) demonstrates how this works:

Planning Book Mockup

	Key Figure Name	Common Order Categories	10/5/12	10/12/12	10/19/12	10/26/12	11/2/12	11/9/12
Demand	Forecast		5,000	1,000	300	400	800	900
	Sales Order		5,500	-	-	-	-	-
	Distribution Demand	Unconfirmed Purchase Requisition (either internal or external source of supply)			1,200			
	Distribution Demand Confirmed	Confirmed Purchase Requisitions or Purchase Orders						
	Dependent Demand							
	Total Demand		**5,500**	**1,000**	**1,500**	400	800	900
Supply	Distribution Receipt	Stock Transport or Purchase Requisition			200			
	Distribution Receipt Confirmed	Stock Transport Orders and Purchase Orders						
	In Transit		500					
	Production Planned		2,800	600	1,300	400	800	900
	Production Confirmed							
	Total Receipts		**3,300**	**600**	**1,500**	400	800	900
Stock	Stock on Hand		1,000	600	600	600	600	600
	Max Stock Level		600	600	600	600	600	600
	Reorder Point		500	500	500	500	500	500
	Safety Stock		500	300	300	300	300	300

This spreadsheet mockup simulates the forward calculating (beyond the replenishment lead time) reorder point in SNP. While there are no sales orders after the first time bucket, there are forecasts in every time bucket and this drives the reorder point-based planned orders into the future. I have also "set" a maximum stock quantity, so APO would therefore manage its planned orders to come in underneath this maximum stock level.

Adjusting the Reorder Point Macro in APO to Not Forward Calculate Beyond the Replenishment Lead Time

While forward calculation was a decision by SAP APO development, it is not necessarily how all clients want to have their reorder points function. In fact, one company that I worked for wanted to have the option of both reorder point calculation methods. The reorder points are set in the planning book based upon a value entered in the product-location master. However, as with all macros, the reorder point macro can be adjusted. In fact, the adjustment that is required for the reorder point macro is quite minor and can be done easily, as is described in the following article:

http://www.scmfocus.com/sapplanning/2012/10/07/forecast-based-forward-calculating-reorder-points/

Conclusion

The explanation of which supply planning methods are used on projects is greatly oversimplified. While a company may say that it is using the optimizer or a heuristic, this may not be the only supply planning method being used in the solution. However, companies have been using a mixed supply planning approach for many years, although the decision about which method to use has traditionally been based upon the system in question—one method is used in the ERP system and another method used in the external planning system. Very little has been written about how to combine supply planning methods in one system, or combine different supply planning methods from multiple external planning supply systems. I have written previously about combining methods or applications. For some time I have promoted the idea of "blending" forecasting applications which have very simple and easy-to-manipulate attribute-based forecasting systems, with those that have weak attribute-based planning functionality, as is described in the following articles:

http://www.scmfocus.com/supplychaininnovation/2010/08/the-benefit-of-blended-solutions-based-upon-component-based-software/

http://www.scmfocus.com/demandplanning/2010/07/using-demandworks-smoothie-for-forecast-prototyping/

http://www.scmfocus.com/demandplanning/2012/02/combining-the-hierarchies-of-two-different-demand-planning-systems/

This book describes using multiple methods of supply planning, but only for the S&OP/MPS/rough cut capacity plan or the initial supply plan. These are the two supply planning threads that receive the majority of emphasis within organizations, and for which the most methods and most method modifiers have been developed. These supply planning threads also have the same methods available to them, with the primary differences being things like the time horizon that is applied or the portion of the product database which is processed. These topics are covered in detail in my book *S&OP, MPS and Rough Cut Capacity Planning in Software*. When describing the method being used, it is also necessary to describe the method modifier being employed. This is particularly true when referring to the SNP heuristic.

This chapter explained the different alternatives that can be assigned to a product-location combination in SAP SNP (but which also apply to many other supply planning systems). These options are a combination of methods and method modifiers. Companies often select a method without understanding the implications. Because the multi method approach (within a single application) described in this book is not well publicized, many companies do not realize that they have a wider pallet of supply planning options.

The lengthy conversations regarding the merits of various supply planning methods and modifiers over others belie the fact that there is no one method that is best for every situation. A better conversation might be to discuss when each option is appropriate and how to get the multiple options to effectively work together.

In addition to the standard methods and modifiers, adjustments can be made to modifier calculations. These adjustments increase the available alternatives and detract from the argument for planning some products in SAP ERP. A good example of this is reorder point, which was covered in this chapter.

CHAPTER 3

Combining Supply Planning Methods Across External Planning Systems and ERP Systems

A common question that arises when implementing an external supply chain planning system is what portion of the product-location database should be planned in the ERP system, and what part of the product-location database should be planned in the external planning system. Let's say that the design for an implementation was to place the critical products into the advanced planning system and the noncritical products into the ERP system to be planned with simpler methods. The products that were planned in the advanced planning systems would normally meet one of the following criteria:

- The product is critical
- The product is forecastable
- The product has a long lead time
- The product is capacity-constrained
- The product is a high-margin item
- The product is a high-visibility item or is responsible for cross demand for other items

- The product is a finished good and independent demand item (as opposed to dependent demand item a semi-finished or component)

There is considerable background as to how companies make the decision about which products to plan using the advanced planning system, and in order to understand the decision it is important to review the history of implementations of external supply chain planning systems.

A Trip Down Memory Lane

When advanced planning systems were first introduced, and for some time thereafter, it became the standard operating procedure to divide the product database into critical products and noncritical products. Critical products were those with either or both long lead times and constraints, and which consumed the most time from planners.

Focus On SAP's Position with the Split Product Database

Planning some products in ERP and others in the external planning system is an approach that originated from some of the earliest companies in advanced planning, such as i2 Technologies and Manugistics. Like many other approaches, it was copied by SAP. Prior to having their own planning system, SAP was in favor of planning most products in SAP ERP, a recommendation that had little to do with effective or ineffective design, and much to do with power and commercial implications. SAP's strategy maximized their leverage and power on projects.

However, after SAP developed their own external planning application and after they had saturated their customer base with their ERP system, SAP's financial incentives changed and their opinion of what was "right" changed as well. This is the problem with listening to vendors: only in very rare circumstances will you get a scientific answer to a question—an answer that is unpolluted by the sales side of the company. Currently, SAP's main thrust is to sell more products to their customers by migrating them away ERP. For example, they have taken some business processes that don't have much to do with planning, such as warehouse management, and placed them into SCM with the Extended Warehouse Management module. SCM is the umbrella term for all advanced planning modules. To learn more about SAP's evolving terminology with respect to advanced planning and SCM, please refer to the following article:

http://www.scmfocus.com/sapplanning/2009/05/15/sap-scm-vs-apo/

Most people that work in supply chain planning software are aware that the approach described above is the traditional or standard way of deciding what products to plan in the ERP system and what products to plan in the external planning system. However, many people do not know that the reason for this division in the first place was, very simply, hardware limitations. When external planning systems were first introduced, hardware had just developed to the point that it could handle the complex processing requirements of more advanced planning methods. However, this did not mean that hardware had developed to the point where advanced planning methods were economical to use for the entire product-location database. When researching supply planning methods for my book on inventory optimization, I found that supply planning has been repeatedly marked by the development of planning methods that are too computationally intensive to be run on the hardware of the day. However, as time passed and computing power became available, the methods that were once only to be found in a research paper were finally commercialized into enterprise software.

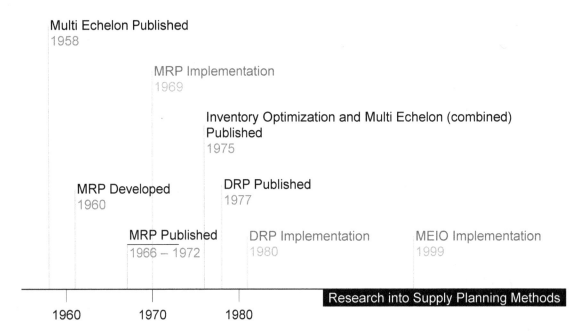

This graphic shows the history of the development of some of the most popular supply planning methods in software today.

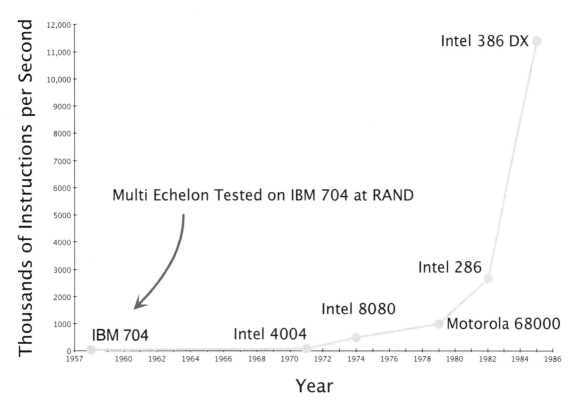

This chart stops at 1986; the sheer magnitude of the developments after 1986 would make the earlier data points imperceptible. A relationship that is not shown in this graphic, but which should be recognized, is the price of the hardware. The first data point is the IBM 704, a specialized computer designed for engineering and scientific calculation. The computer filled a large room and was connected to multiple printers, at least four tape drives (and up to ten), a magnetic drum as big as a refrigerator, and a dot matrix printer, card punch and (punched) card reader all of which were the size of present-day washing machines. Only one hundred and twenty-three IBM 704s were ever purchased over a six-year period, and only universities and government-supported research institutions tended to buy them. Meanwhile, the later data points represent processors that were sold as part of personal computers. Therefore, the cost-to-performance chart would be even more impressive than this graphic.

Chart developed with data from Wikipedia:

http://en.wikipedia.org/wiki/Instructions_per_second

Focus On  Dated Methods in Supply Chain Planning

As can be seen by the previous chart, one's strategy needs to evolve to take advantage of the very significant advances in computing power. Like many areas, the common or popular approach lags the available technologies. Many companies still implement forecasting software with a dated ROLAP (Relational On Line Analytical Processing) design, which greatly limits their ability to gain access to attribute-based forecasting. More details on this specific issue are described in the link below:

http://www.scmfocus.com/demandplanning/2012/03/why-not-all-attribute-and-rolap-solutions-are-equal/

In the area of BOM management, several of the books available discuss the importance of flattening the BOM, something that is quite unnecessary if one has a BOM management system. A good deal of my book, *The Bill of Materials in Excel, ERP, Planning and PLM/BMMS Software,* is dedicated to explaining how to leverage modern software to manage the BOM entirely differently than the dated way used by the vast majority of companies today.

http://www.scmfocus.com/scmfocuspress/select-a-book/the-software-approaches-for-improving-your-bill-of-materials-book/

The Disadvantages of Splitting the Product Database Between ERP and the External Planning System

It turns out that there are many costs or disadvantages to splitting the product database between multiple systems. These disadvantages are not frequently discussed and I have not been able to find published documents that explain these disadvantages. Therefore, I am unsure as to how well these disadvantages are disseminated, much less understood. I have listed them below:

1. *Multiple Systems and Training and Familiarity:* The split approach requires more work, overhead and training, as planners must use two systems instead of one.
2. *The Enhanced User Interface Capabilities of External Planning Systems:* Planners must use the less sophisticated user interface of the ERP system versus using the more modern user interface the of external planning system.

    http://www.scmfocus.com/supplyplanning/2011/06/27/product-database-segmentation-between-erp-and-external-supply-planning-systems/

3. *The Reporting Implications:* To report planning results, two systems must be queried. (The ERP system would naturally receive the planning results of the external planning system, but this is still a more complex approach than reporting exclusively from one system.)

In order to facilitate decision-making on this topic, I have included the matrix on the following page:

	Planning in both the ERP and External Planning System	Planning Everything in the External Planning System
More Consultants are Familiar with the Approach	Yes	No
Better Planner Efficiency	No	Yes
Easier Reporting	No	Yes
Access to More Method Modifiers	Yes	No(but can be rectified with macro adjustment)
Hardware Requirements	This is a complicated question. It depends upon whether a multi method approach is followed -- with simpler methods being used for a portion of the product location database.	
Lower Training Costs	No	Yes

Multiple Systems and Training and Familiarity

Companies and planners prefer to train their planners on one system rather than two, as one system is more efficient. The efficiency of the planner's overall performance decreases if the planner must access more systems in order to obtain the required information. Some vendors like to simplify the issue down to whether or not the user needs to sign in only once to access all the information they need. However, this is not simply a matter of a single or dual login, but a feature of gaining familiarity with one system.

The Enhanced User Interface Capabilities of External Planning Systems

External planning systems will always have better user interfaces than the ERP system. Planning is only one aspect of what an ERP system does, while planning is the only thing an external planning system does. Therefore, a divided strategy will result in planners spending more time using the system with a weaker user interface. Compare the Stock Requirements List (which is a view in SAP ERP) with the Product View, which resides in SAP APO. I have inserted screen shots of both views below and on the following page:

Basic information in this ERP View

Stock/Requirements List as of 15:13 hrs

A	Date	MRP element	MRP element data	Reschedulin	E	Receipt/Re	Available Qty	Sto	Vendor	Vendor name
	05.10.2012	Stock					500.009.378			
	25.07.2012	POItem	4500000229/00010		20	10	500.009.388	1020	300000	Vendor domestic
	25.07.2012	CusOrd	0000000261/000010/0...			5-	500.009.383			
	25.07.2012	CusOrd	0000000266/000010/0...			50-	500.009.333			
	26.07.2012	CusOrd	0000000268/000010/0...			20-	500.009.313			
	27.07.2012	CusOrd	0000000270/000010/0...			364.000-	499.645.313	1020		
	30.07.2012	CusOrd	0000000271/000010/0...			20-	499.645.293			
	30.07.2012	CusOrd	0000000274/000020/0...			20-	499.645.273			
	30.07.2012	CusOrd	0000000275/000020/0...			20-	499.645.253			
	01.08.2012	CusOrd	0000000279/000010/0...			20-	499.645.233			
	03.08.2012	CusOrd	0000000280/000020/0...			5-	499.645.228	1020		
	06.08.2012	CusOrd	0000000277/000010/0...			20-	499.645.208			
	06.08.2012	CusOrd	0000000278/000010/0...			20-	499.645.188			
	06.08.2012	CusOrd	0000000278/000020/0...			20-	499.645.168			
	07.08.2012	FOCDly	0000000287/000010/0...			5-	499.645.163			
	08.08.2012	CusOrd	0000000296/000010/0...			5-	499.645.158			
	09.08.2012	POItem	4500000232/00010		20	1.000	499.646.158	1020	300000	Vendor domestic
	13.08.2012	CusOrd	0000000288/000010/0...			5-	499.646.153			
	13.08.2012	CusOrd	0000000289/000010/0...			1-	499.646.152			

Page   1 / 2

Peggings selection

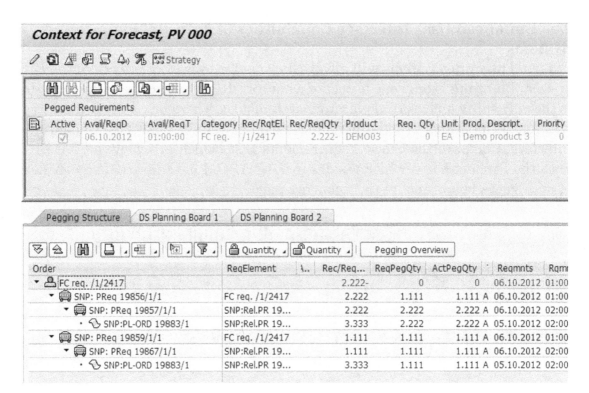

Both of these views provide similar information, but the Product View is much more powerful and multifaceted. (Although it's not an elite user interface design, it is simply much better than the similar view in SAP ERP). SAP APO has something that SAP ERP does not have: the Product View can show more detail on peggings. A "pegging" is a connection between a supply element and a demand element. While a pegging is a single connection between demand and supply, a chain of peggings can show the connection between a purchase requisition at the end of the supply network and a sales order or forecast at the very top of the supply network.

 **Demand to Supply Pegging**

Peggings are very important for a variety of reasons. Pegging allows a planner to trace the set of demand and supply connections between different echelons within the supply network, including the initial demand (sales order or forecast), all of the stock transport requisitions, and all of the planned (production) orders and the purchase requisitions.

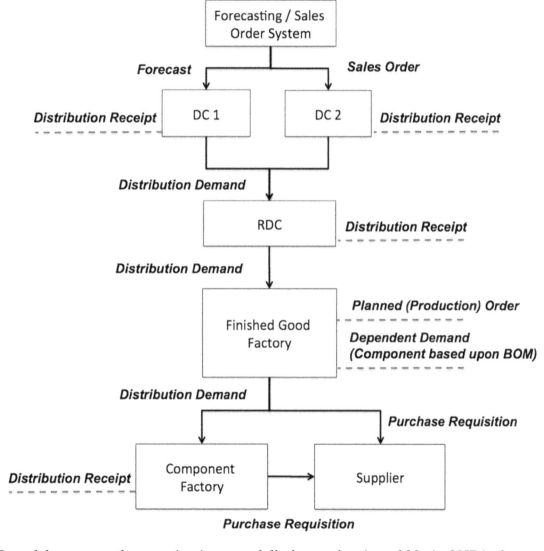

The Supply Network Flow

One of the reasons that pegging is not as fully featured as it could be in SNP is that pegging is a bit onerous to check one by one. This is why some companies toy with the idea *of extracting all of the peggings from SNP and placing them into a report making them easier to extract. However, peggings cannot be easily extracted from APO. The peggings are not stored in a table (for some strange reason which is not apparent to me) but is stored in liveCache—APO's memory / hierarchical database. Unlike a table, LiveCache cannot be directly queried, and for specific items for which customers have requested information, SAP has created a series of BAPIs (Business Application Programming Interface), which allow the extraction to be performed. However, once extracted the peggings cannot be directly used with ease, but must be filtered through a program which can convert many of the system codes (SYSIDs, etc.) into a format that can be read by humans and placed into some type of report. Peggings are updated when a supply method is applied. In many implementations, this update occurs nightly. It makes good sense to extract the peggings after this run is complete so that the planners have updated pegging information in their pegging report at the beginning of the day.*

Overall it's a hassle, but there is no other way to get this type of information from the system. For those who are particularly interested in the topic of peggings, the vendor Manugistics makes their peggings easy to obtain in a variety of ways, right within the application, without the necessity for any coding.

The pegging report is shown conceptually on the following page:

Tracing the Purchase Order to the Sales Order

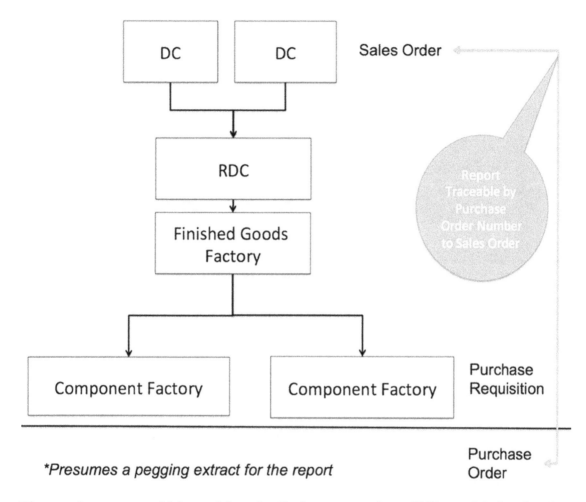

*Presumes a pegging extract for the report

The pegging report, which would work off of an extract from SNP, would give the planner a lot of flexibility when checking the peggings. For example, the planner could select all of the peggings that met various search criteria, allowing the planner to much more quickly move through their activities.

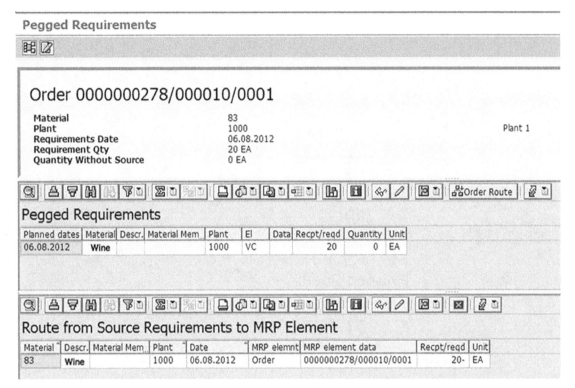

Peggings exist in ERP systems as well, as the screen shot above demonstrates. The peggings can be arrived at by selecting a line item and then selecting the pegging button at the bottom of the Stock Requirements List.

Peggings that are created inside of SAP APO are not shown in the Stock Requirements List in SAP ERP and vice versa. The pegging view in ERP is designed to show peggings that are created by a procedure (such as MRP) within the ERP system.

Reporting Implications

Very simply, it is more expensive and more complicated for a company to pull extracts from two systems rather than one. In addition, fewer reports are necessary with one system. With two systems, the number of reports required to provide the organization with an overall picture of the plan is higher, as data must be extracted and reported on from both systems. With one system, some of the reporting requirements can be met by simply using the user interface of the external planning system. For instance, when I want to view total system inventory in SNP, I can simply create a selection profile for all products at all locations in the planning book (easily done with a wildcard) and I can view the overall system inventory by planning bucket for the entire planning horizon.

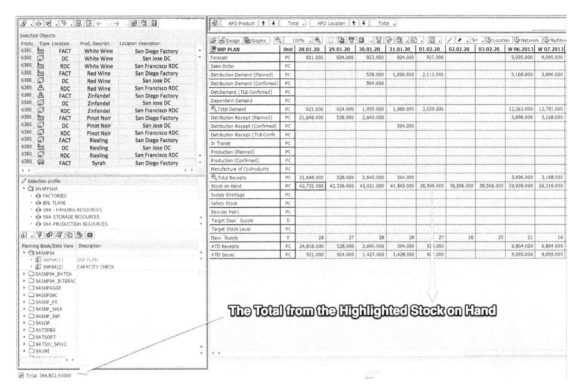

As you can see by selecting all product-location combinations in the selected objects in the upper left pane, you can see the aggregation of key figures to the spreadsheet at the right. This aggregation is for the entire supply network, however, I can show any aggregation subset that I wish by adjusting the selection profile. I can also select one key figure, as I have with the Stock on Hand key figure, and with a right mouse click I can select to sum all of the values that I have selected. On the bottom left of the screen, the value will be summed. When doing this, the options are:

1. *Total*
2. *Mean Value*
3. *Maximum*
4. *Minimum*
5. *User-Specified Function*
6. *Number of Filled Cells*

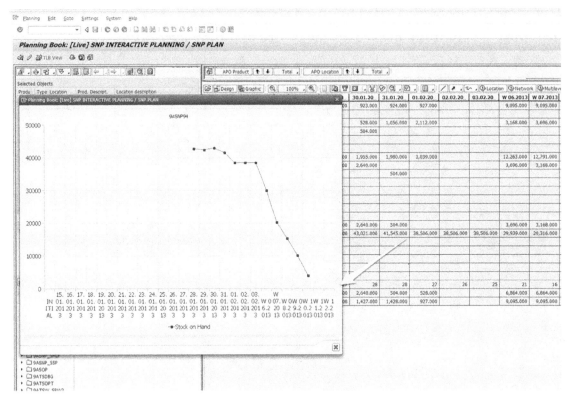

With one key figure selected, a graphic can be shown by right mouse clicking and selecting graphic. SAP creates a rudimentary graphic, which can be used to find issues more quickly than looking at a row of values.

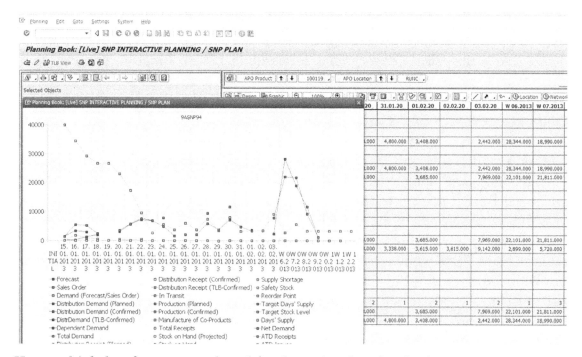

Here multiple key figures are selected for the entire planning horizon.

A split approach will only give me the inventory for products planned in SAP APO. I then have to figure out how to do an inventory report in ERP, and then add up the two values to arrive at the total system inventory. I would then need to do it for the exact planning bucket for which I wanted to find inventory information. Even this simple example means more work.

A split strategy will require that more reports be written. An additional problem for many companies is that they use SAP Business Warehouse (BW) as their reporting system, and BW reports have a habit of showing up late. In fact, I have yet to see BW reports that appear within six months of the APO go-live, and they typically trail the APO implementation by over a year.

http://www.scmfocus.com/scmbusinessintelligence/2011/07/the-amazing-disappearing-bi-reports/

Beyond being late, I have yet to see an implementation where BW reports were used frequently. SAP reporting is filled with promises, but will always under-deliver, so going with a design that relies upon BW to function properly is an extremely dubious approach.

Gaining Access to SAP ERP Method Modifiers

Another reason to split the product database is to gain access to the way that the method modifiers work in SAP ERP. While one would think that only non-SAP external planning vendors would decline to offer the standard modifiers available within SAP ERP, this is not the case. For some reason, when SAP developed APO, they did not simply add to the method modifiers that already existed in ERP (which I think would have been a better approach).[2] Instead they seemed to start with a blank slate. Now, when companies implement APO, they are forced to abandon method modifiers that have worked for them for years and move to the modifier calculation methods in APO. This has been a motivator for companies to keep more of their products in the ERP system. For several reasons, SAP altered how the basic modifier settings work in APO, thus causing confusion for companies that are familiar with using settings as they are in ERP. One very good example of this is the reorder point, but the issue applies to other modifiers such as the day's supply. However, method modifiers—which are typically calculated within planning books in something called macros—can be adjusted without a great deal of work to match the calculation basis that is used in SAP ERP (primarily by deactivating steps within the macro).

---

[2] It would have made less sense to migrate the methods from SAP ERP (MRP and DRP) over to APO as companies move toward APO in order to leverage more advanced methods. However, the same cannot be said for method modifiers. SAP could have very easily included all of the same modifier calculation methods available in ERP, and then simply added on to them. The ease of macro adjustments to the modifier macros shows how easy it would have been for SAP development to ship the APO this way as a standard.

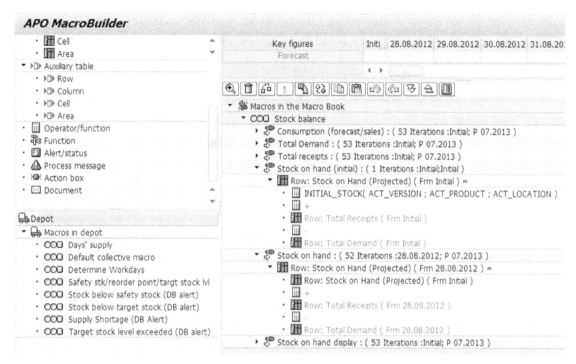

This is the reorder point macro in APO. This macro can be adjusted by simply removing several steps, changing the macro from the calculation basis that is used for the reorder point in SAP APO to how it functions in SAP ERP. Both macro calculation bases can be used in APO but not for the same product locations. It means creating two separate planning books. Product-location combinations are then assigned to the planning books with the correct basis.

This adjustment enables a company to migrate its ERP modifiers to APO and to plan all products in a single system.

Conclusion

Many companies and consultants divide the product database so that critical products are planned in SAP APO while noncritical products are planned in SAP ERP. However, they do so without understanding that the original logic for this rule of thumb was formed in a time when hardware capabilities were more limited than they are today.

The standard method of dividing the product database into critical and non-critical items is now dated due to major advancements in computational power. Interestingly, I have yet to meet a supply planning consultant who knows the original reason for the split database approach, meaning that the split approach is still described to companies as a best practice. People who have no background in advanced planning, but are able to influence the decision-making process also accept the split approach as gospel, such as an SAP account manager I worked with who was sure this was a good approach, but could not explain why. I recently worked with an account director at SAP who was a high-level project management type, who told the client, "You always plan some items in APO and some in ERP."

Secondly, the costs of the split approach are almost always underestimated if they are mentioned at all. SAP ERP is "stable," which in developer-speak means that it is not seeing much further development. SAP APO not only has superior planning functionality vis-à-vis SAP ERP, but has a better planning user interface as well. Planning all products with SAP APO means far fewer reports, as the necessity to reconcile between APO and ERP is eliminated—always a good thing, but particularly important when BW is the report application.

SAP development made the strange decision of not including the exact calculation basis for each method modifier as a baseline in APO. As a result, companies either had to transition to APO's calculation basis (often not what they wanted) or keep their products being planned in APO. However, adjusting the modifier macros can rectify this situation. In cases where companies want to use both the standard modifier macro and the adjusted modifier macro, it is necessary to create multiple planning books, as each planning book can only contain one type of macro calculation per modifier key figure.

CHAPTER 4

Preparing for the Prototype for Multi Method Testing

Prototyping is described in detail in Chapter 5: "Prototyping the Multi Method Supply Planning Model." However, before we get to that, it's necessary to cover some foundational information so that the prototype can be properly understood.

Prototyping to Obtain the Highest Quality Business Input

Building prototypes in APO allows a business to see how the various alternatives will work in SNP, and thus supporting them in making their decisions and in filling out the product-location spreadsheet database. A common error made by APO consultants is to attempt to interpret requirements without letting the business users into the process to choose for themselves. Instead, the role of the module consultant should be to expose the alternatives to the business, and for the business to feel sufficiently educated to the point they can make the decisions themselves. Prototyping is one of the most important methods of bringing the business into the decision-making process.

Assuming that the customer wants decisions made for them is actually a common problem among providers in service industries. For example, surveys have shown that doctors routinely assume that a higher percentage of patients want their treatment decisions make for them than actually do. I have had this experience dealing with physicians; it seems that if I ask too many questions they keep some of the logic as to how they arrived at their conclusions to themselves.

Talking about physicians leads us to the topic of solution socialization. Because many consultants are simply not that interested in the task, they end up keeping many of the particulars of the decision-making process to themselves. Then when the implementation goes live, the business does not support or understand the configuration. Socializing the solution is the focus of the following article:

http://www.scmfocus.com/inventoryoptimizationmultiechelon/2011/05/
socializing-supply-chain-optimization/

Setting up the Demo Map

Before selecting a variety of supply planning methods and method modifiers, it is necessary to test them out by creating a number of scenarios in a prototype or demonstration environment. Configuring the necessary settings, as well as setting up the necessary transactions, is one part of the challenge, but another is to develop a graphic that allows the audience of the demonstration system to understand where they are in the model. I have come to call this the demo map. Not only is the demo map valuable for presenting the demonstration system, but, when created as an overview of the proposed design before the actual prototype is built, can assist the application specialists in setting up the demonstration or prototype. Therefore, it is just as valuable at the beginning of the demo process— during conceptualization, as it as the end, during demonstration.

The Demo Map

The demo map should accomplish the following objectives:

Introduction to the Demo Map		
Question	Answer Number	Answers
What is the Purpose of the Demo Map?	1	Provide the audience with the ability to follow the demo through various product locations in the supply network.
	2	Explain what is being done in each step of the demo.
How Does the Demo Map Work?	1	Follow the yellow box, which is set behind the product location combination which is being demonstrated in the system.
	2	Look for the orange text which explains what is covered in each demo step.

The demo map explanation can be used to introduce the demo map to the audience. There is quite a bit of information in the demo map. Demo maps are rarely used, so it is very likely that your audience will not have seen one before. The demo map should be introduced and explained in order to get the maximum effect from using it.

The approach used in the demo map that I have shown should be considered. The demo map shows the following:

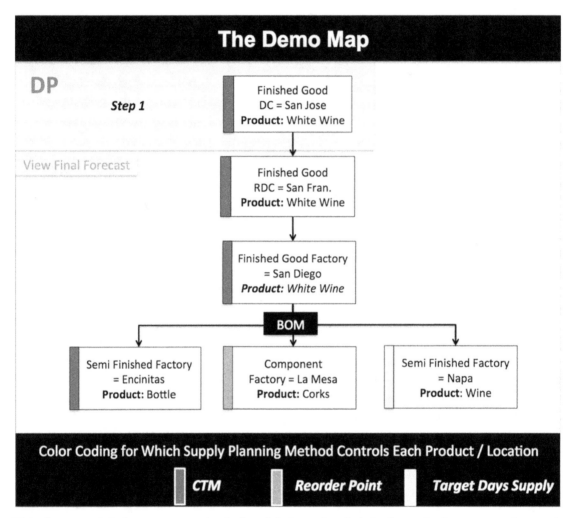

This is a model that stops a single level below the finished goods factory, so it can be shown on one slide legibly. However, with bigger networks, the slide must typically be quite long (which can be accomplished by going into Page Setup in PowerPoint and choosing any aspect ratio that you want).

Above you can see that through the overall network, we follow just one finished good. "Step 1" begins in a different application—SAP DP. The business wants to see demos integrated among all the different applications. Therefore, one of the important pieces of information to give them is what application they are going to be looking at.

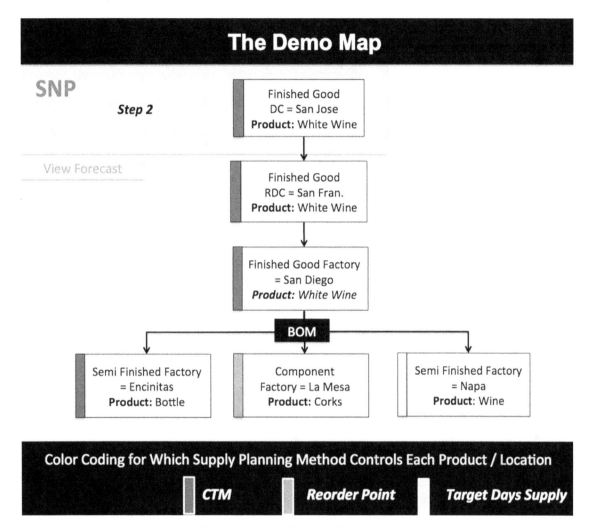

The next step of viewing the forecast in SNP, it delineates for the audience the difference between the DP and SNP planning books. After showing this slide, we would go into the application in the planning book and show the forecast.

Along the bottom of the slide, there is a color-coding, which matches colored boxes added to the side of every product-location combination. This coding lets the audience know how each product location is being planned. In this book, these color differences will show up as shadings.

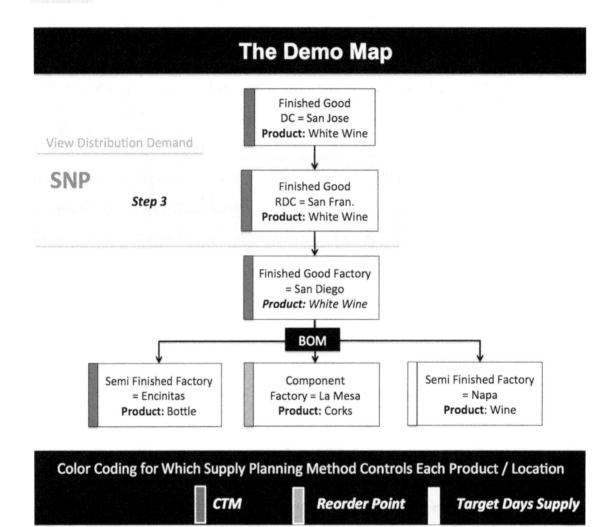

Now we follow the network flow to the RDC. The demand is passed to the regional distribution center as an unconfirmed stock transport requisition, and shows up as a distribution demand at the RDC. After this slide, we would select the location in the planning book and show the distribution demand.

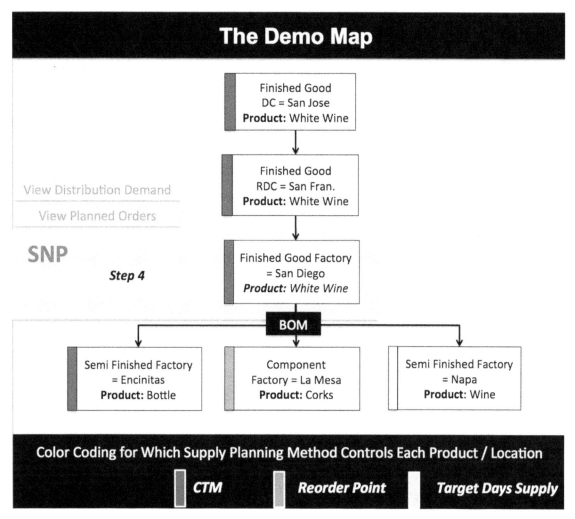

Now we follow the network flow to the finished goods factory. This factory receives demand from the RDC as distribution demand, but creates planned orders—which are planned production orders.

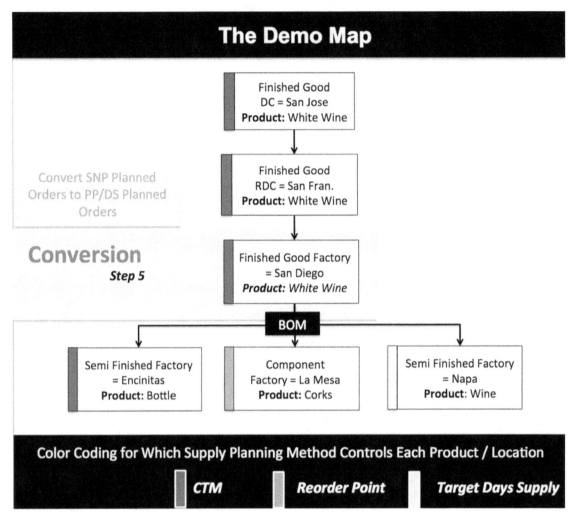

While we don't move way from the location, we pass the SNP planned orders to PP/DS by converting them, so that PP/DS can perform detailed scheduling.

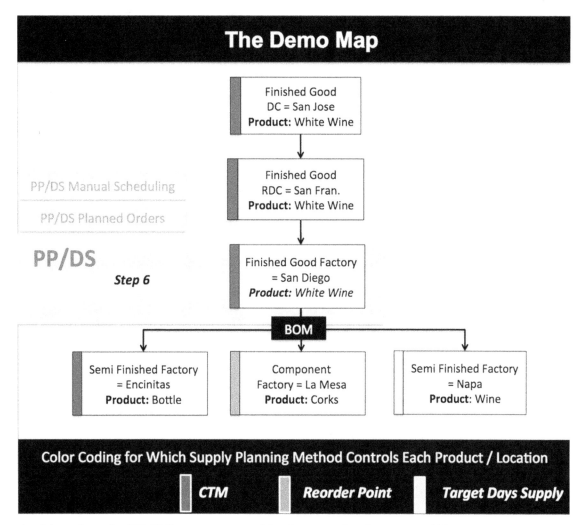

At this point, the PP/DS resource would take over the demo, possibly run a PP/DS heuristic and go into the detailed scheduling board, to show how the planned order could be moved around.

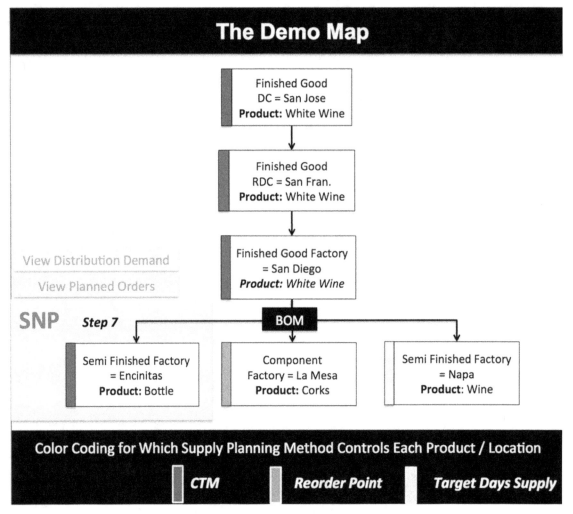

At this point the demo would be handed back to the SNP resource, and we could check the distribution demand and the planned orders at the bottle plant.

Hopefully that provides some insight of how to set up and use a demo map. After having used a demo map for several demonstrations, I have some observations about how to best use the demo map:

1. It is extremely beneficial if there can be two screens/projectors in the presentation room. This way, the demo map can always be displayed on one screen, while the SAP screens are displayed on the other.

2. The demonstration should always have to people driving each of the project-ing computers. This way the resource that is driving SAP does not have to worry about also moving through the slides in the demo map.

3. Complex demos of this nature (the example I have shown has been simplified for this book), and often tend to drag a bit as the SAP resources are moving through the screens and explaining the functionality. When things do drag, it is beneficial to have someone from the business, who has also worked along the SAP resources, to come in and provide some color commentary.

Documenting the Prototype/Demo Matrix

In addition to testing the methods using a prototype, it is vital to document the results of the multiple scenarios that are tested. This important step has a strong overlay or intersection with simulation, as described in the article below:

http://www.scmfocus.com/sapplanning/2009/11/08/scm-simulation-archival-blog/

What this means is that the results of the various scenarios must be well-documented, allowing for informed decision-making as to which functionalities to enable and which to leave to the side. This spreadsheet maintains all of the important features of the scenario, including the "decision" that results from each test. Prototypes that are documented in this manner make the design easy to follow, a necessary adjunct to blueprint documentation. Blueprint documentation often explains what has been decided, but lacks the layers and explanation that is found in the matrix shown on the previous page. An experienced resource in the application can read through a prototype matrix and quickly understand the various things that the project was interested in testing.

Configuring the Method Profiles and the Method Modifiers on the Product-Location Master

Up until this point, we have primarily discussed documenting the configuration and parameter data in external spreadsheets. However, the options that we choose must be placed into the supply planning system in order to build a prototype. Much foundational configuration must be completed to arrive at an operational model, including tasks such as setting up storage bucket profiles, planning bucket profiles and creating the planning objects structures. However, getting input from the business on many of the foundational objects for the configuration does not consume very much time, so in this chapter I will focus on two things:

1. The method profiles
2. Setting up the product-location master fields

Configuring the Method Profiles

Configuring the major methods in SNP means going into SNP's own configuration area. This means going to the SNP heuristic, CTM or to the SNP optimizer. One example of this is shown below:

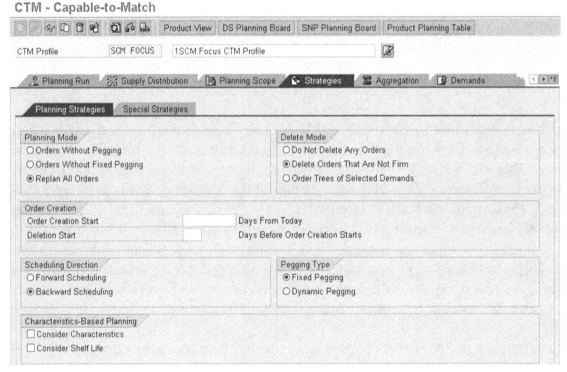

This is one configuration screen of CTM (CTM has many configuration screens).

Setting up the Method Modifiers
In addition to all the other settings that are product-location specific, the method modifiers are set in the product-location master. Here are all of the tabs in the product-location master that are relevant for SNP.

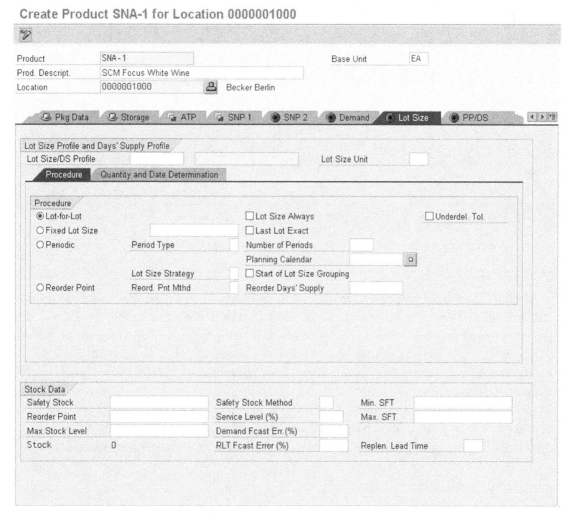

These lot size tabs control the order batching in the system and whether a reorder point will control the supply planning for a particular product location. There are also controls for safety stock.

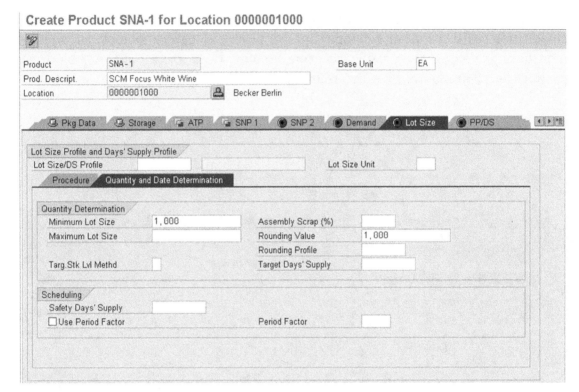

In this tab, the target stock level method can be enabled. A target stock level is entered into this field. There are a variety of methods for generating the target stock level. For instance, target stock level is a main integration point between inventory optimization, multi echelon software, and more basic software like SAP SNP. The target stock level can be determined in a variety of complex ways, or of course in very simple ways, as described in the following article:

http://www.scmfocus.com/supplyplanning/2012/08/24/integrating-a-preexisting-target-stock-level-with-different-supply-planning-methods/

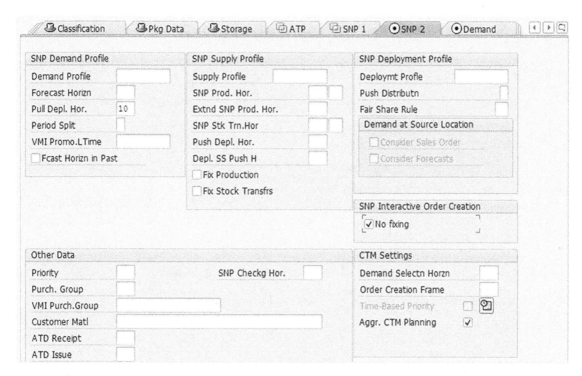

Many of the timing settings are on this tab. The timing settings tell the application how far to look into the future in order to perform different planning functions. A few of these settings are shown on the following page, and compared and contrasted with other settings.

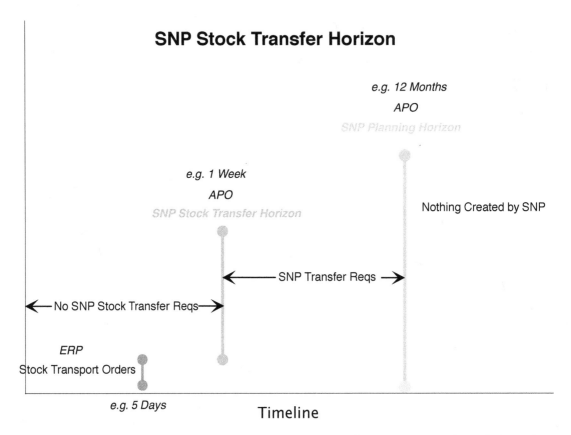

For a complete explanation of the timing settings in four modules of APO (DP, SNP, GATP and PP/DS), see my book, Planning Horizons and Timings in SAP APO.

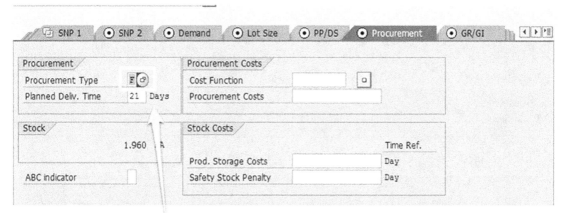

These tabs must be populated from the product-location spreadsheet, which allows every product-location combination to be treated differently.

Each method in SAP SNP is implemented through the configuration of "profiles." CTM and the optimizer have profiles, and the SNP heuristic has variants. I will refer to them as profiles as they are essentially identical in purpose, and this makes it easier to discuss them along with the other profiles. All of these method profiles are preconfigured groups of settings that control how to run each of the methods. Because the SNP heuristic is the simplest, it has the fewest settings.

Profiles can be copied into new profiles, which is a very effective way to control the quality of the planning runs. This is particularly valuable with the CTM and optimizer profiles that have a tremendous number of settings. In fact, the various profiles in the system that are used for planning runs constitute a major component of the intellectual property that has come from the implementation.

Each of the profiles has fields that control the master data selection for which the method is to be applied. For instance, if we look at the master data selection for the SNP heuristic, we can see those specific fields for both product and locations.

Supply Network Planning: Planning Run

| ⊕ | 🗐 | Display Logs |

Data Source

Planning Book	9ASNP94
Data View	SNP94 (1)
Global SNP Settings Profile	SAP
Paral. Proc. Profile	

◉ Entire Planning Horizon
○ Planning Horizon in Days   0

Object Selection

○ Selection Profile

    Selection Profile   🔍

◉ Manual Selection

Planning Version	000		
Product Number	Red Wine	to		➡
Location	San Jose DC	to		➡
Low-Level Code		to		➡

Scope of Planning

◉ Network (Heuristic)
○ Location (Heuristic)
☑ Take into account found components in planning run
☑ Add products from supersession chains
☐ Net Change Planning

| Source Determination | All Levels | 🗎 |
| Temporary Low-Level Codes | Do not use temporary low-level codes | 🗎 |

In the situation where all product-location combinations are planned by a single method, "plan all products and all locations" can be selected and applied. This is also the traditional setting when running the application in prototype or demo mode. However, when multiple supply planning methods are used, each profile will only include a subset of the overall products and locations. At the most elementary level, a big decision of the project is to determine which product locations will be run with each method. To do so, product locations must be segmented into the different major methods, and settings must be inter-related with the product- location master, which has two minor methods as well as the four moderating control settings. The product-location database spreadsheet and the product-location master are explained in the next chapter.

Reorder Point, TSL, TDS, Max Stock Level, and Lot Size and Major Supply Planning Methods						
(Major) Planning Method	Reorder Point	Target Stock Level	Target Days Supply	Maximum Stock Level	Lot Size (Units)	Period Lot Size
SNP Heuristic	X	X	X	X	X	X
Capable to Match						
SNP Optimizer				X	X	

In the matrix above, the method is documented per product location. As you can see, the reorder point and the target stock level (TSL) only work with the SNP heuristic and are ignored by CTM and the optimizer. An important consideration for determining when to use one supply planning method over another is whether the product-location combination is forecastable. More on this topic is available at the link below:

http://www.scmfocus.com/demandplanning/2010/06/forecastable-non-forecastable-formula/

The above matrix can be used to help explain how to make selections between the various supply planning methods. Once this has been explained, the business subject matter experts can go off and code the entire product-location database for each method that is used.

There is much more to a successful configuration than simply assigning product locations to profiles and then running the profiles. There is a sequence in which the profiles of the different methods must be run in order for the system to work properly. As such, testing must be performed to make the desired assignments between the supply planning method and the product-location combination workable and to set up the profiles in the proper sequence. We will get into all of the detail on this topic in the following chapter.

Background on the Configuration of Multiple Supply Planning Methods

Once a company decides to use multiple supply planning methods, the next question is how to implement this in the system's configuration. How to do this is not widely understood or even explained. I believe this book is one of the first to describe how to implement multiple supply planning methods in the configuration of any external supply chain planning system.

It would be most convenient if using multiple supply planning methods could simply be accomplished by assigning every product location a supply planning method and have the supply plan be created in a logical and consistent manner.

Unfortunately, making multiple methods work together is a good deal more complex than this because of how APO was developed. In this chapter, I will describe how combining multiple methods can be accomplished with the following methods and method modifiers:

1. Capable to Match (CTM)
2. The SNP Heuristic with:
   a. A Reorder Point
   b. A Target Stock Level
   c. A Target Days' Supply

The same principle and testing as discussed in this chapter applies to collaboratively using other supply planning methods; however, for any SNP heuristic method modifiers (reorder point, target stocking level, target days supply), either of the other two modifiers (target stock level or target days' supply) could be set the same way as the reorder point I describe here. Within SNP there are several ways of setting up a reorder point, target stock level or target days supply. For the purposes of this demonstration, I will show the most basic settings for each.

Here is a screenshot showing the reorder point as set in the product-location master.

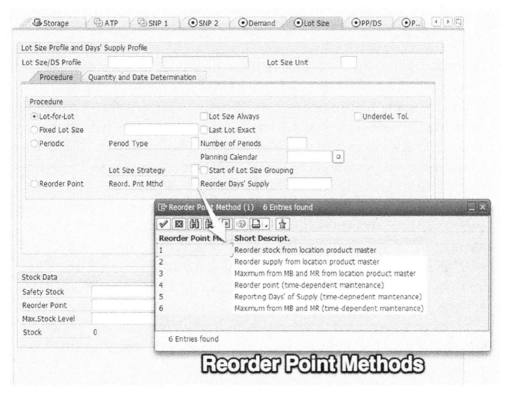

There are six different reorder point settings in SNP.[3] *However, for our purposes, there is no need to use anything but the simplest method, which is where the reorder point macro in the planning book calls on the reorder point as entered as a unit quantity in the product-location master. The time-dependent maintenance reorder points are used when the company has an interest in allowing planners to alter the reorder point per time*

---

[3] Now I am referring to the settings that reorder point uses for its determination, or should I say the alternatives presented in the product location master. This is distinct from the calculation basis of the reorder point, which I covered in Chapter 2: "The Different Supply Planning Methods Available within SAP SNP."

bucket along the time horizon. Time-dependent maintenance allows for a great deal of control over the reorder point, but is also a maintenance item.

On an actual project, it is important to provide all of the alternatives for each setting that are within the scope of the project, which was covered in Chapter 6: "Coding the Product-Location Database/Spreadsheet."

Setting up the Prototype

In setting up this demonstration, I thought it important to keep to some basic rules:

1. There should be three echelons to the supply network. I could have had more, but I could not have had less becuase it is important to be able to see how different supply planning methods function through three layers. One can put any number of echelons into a prototype, but three is sufficient to prove whether or not various supply planning methods can work with one another.
2. Every different permutation that is to be tested will have its own product. This is an important consideration for actual prototypes on projects, the reason being that creating more products enables one to create a planning output without deleting the same planning output in order to test a new scenario. The disadvantage to this is when a number of scenarios are created, as it is necessary to use a production data structure (PDS). This means that the materials must be created in SAP ERP, as well as the routings and the BOMs and the work centers. This can be a good amount of work. For this prototype, I did not set up a production source of supply (no PDS and no PPM). The production supply is, therefore, unconstrained, and SNP will still create planned orders in the factory.
3. I need to create three materials (White Wine, Red Wine, Zinfandel). These three materials would be planned through the top three echelons of the supply network (DC, Regional DC, Finished Goods Factory). Each product would have a different method sequence. This way we can test the all the different scenarios where two methods (reorder point and CTM) are used to plan each echelon.
4. After each run, (and each CTM or heuristic run was assigned to one echelon) the results were checked to see if the correct planning output was generated.

5. A final CTM run was used, which we called a pegging run. This pegging run was not designed to create any new orders, but to simply peg existing supply and demand in the supply network that was created from previous runs. I discuss the pegging run in detail further on in this section. This final CTM run turns out to be the "secret sauce" that enables the methods to perform their planning independently, but then to be tied together with pegging relationships.

Understanding the Planning Book

We will look at several user interfaces in SAP APO, including the Planning Book and the product view. In order to appreciate the screen shots that follow, it's important to understand how the Planning Book works and how to read it. For those who are experienced in SNP, you can probably skip this section. On the other hand, as explaining how the Planning Book works is a constant challenge on APO implementations, you may find some material here that can help you better explain it.

The Planning Book Configuration

The Planning Book is made up of key figures (contained in the rows) that intersect with time buckets (the columns). These key figures can be composed of the following items:

- *Single Categories:* For instance, to show a single category of stock in a single Key Figure.

- *Multiple Categories:* For instance, to show multiple categories of stock in a single Key Figure.

- *Calculations of other Key Figures:* These are calculations and functions that include configuration settings in APO. This is called a macro.

Many of the rows that planners see in the Planning Book are actually calculated values. Through normal use of the Planning Book, there is no way to know for sure which key figures are combinations of categories, or which are calculations (macros) that include other key figures.

A number of the macros are standard calculations that ship with APO. For instance, the reorder point key figure is a macro. Any macro can be adjusted, whether it is a custom macro written for a company or a standard macro.

The Importance of Documenting Macros

Macros should be documented because macros are generally difficult to interpret. This is due to the design of the user interface for macros, which is called the APO Macro Builder. Some consultants become quite efficient at writing macros, but the APO Macro Builder is definitely an acquired taste. For those familiar to expression building in Excel or Mat Lab, the macro logic is much more difficult to follow. However, documenting macros is important for explaining the macro to users and business leaders. Documentation is also important to the APO consultant, as opening up and reading the APO Macro Builder requires interpretation every time. Once macros are interpreted into plain English, they are generally easy to understand.

To improve the understanding of these macros, we have described them extensively in the following post:

> http://www.scmfocus.com/sapplanning/2011/06/09/the-planning-book-key-figure-and-macro-definitions/

Understanding the Structures in APO

All of the objects discussed thus far are part of a hierarchy that is necessary in order to make the Planning Book show the results that it does. For ease of understanding, the graphic below shows how macros, key figures, Planning Book, planning area and planning object structure are all related to one another.

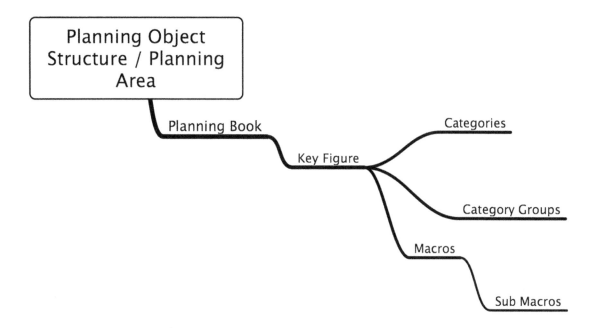

Understanding the Areas of the Planning Book

Before I describe all of the individual components, I would like to review the layout and operation of the SNP Planning Book. The Planning Book is also used for SAP APO Demand Planning (DP). The DP Planning Book has an entirely different layout and different key figures. The end point of the DP Planning Book is the final forecast, while this is the beginning point of the SNP Planning Book. As I will not be focusing on DP, we won't get into the DP Planning Book here. Instead, we will be working backward from the SNP Planning Book as we get into a more and more detailed description of how these values are populated.

The following is a screen shot of the standard SNP Planning Book. This Planning Book can be configured to show some key figures and to hide others based upon the predicted needs of the planners.

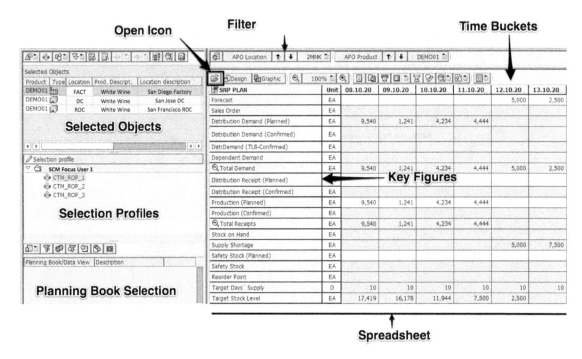

The areas of the Planning Book, marked up above, are explained below:

There are four major areas to the Planning Book:

1. *Planning Book Selection:* The first step in using the Planning Books is to select one to go into. Any number of Planning Books can be created and navigated from the individual Planning Book selection at the bottom left of the Planning Book screen. You can quickly navigate between Planning Books in this area. The Planning Books are stored in folders, which allow them to be categorized. (I don't show any Planning Books in this view, but ordinarily they would be in this location.)

2. *Selection Profiles:* The next step after selecting the specific Planning Book to view is to select an existing selection profile or create a new one. In the selection profile you see in this Planning Book, I have one product (White Wine) and three locations (San Jose, San Francisco, San Diego). Selection Profiles can be assigned to the user ID, so every time the user opens a Planning Book the Selection Profiles will immediately appear. I currently

have three Selection Profiles assigned to my user ID. Each Selection Profile has the same three locations but with a different product (White Wine, Red Wine, Zinfandel). Product-location combinations are the most common selection used in Planning Books, and it is what I used in this prototype. However, APO provides a number of alternatives for what can be viewed in a Planning Book. For instance, a single resource or a group of resources can be brought into the Planning Book in order to check capacity utilization. The different selection profile options are shown further on in this section.

3. *Selected Objects:* Step three in using the Planning Book is to select a single line item, several line items, or all of the objects within the selection profile. This controls what will be displayed in the spreadsheet view to the right. In these screenshots, I select only one object, "combination of a product and location," at a time because I am tracing a single product through the mini-supply network that has been created for this demonstration. However, when the Planning Book is used at companies, selecting multiple line items allows for the planner to see an aggregated view in the values to the right. The values are aggregated, however, when a particular cell is double-clicked or right mouse clicked. The detail view will appear at the bottom, and it is then evident which orders are related to which product and location. Selecting all of the line items, and then clicking the folder or open icon (which brings the values for the selected items into the spreadsheet) allows the Planning Book to be used as a broad reporting tool. In the past, I have created a selection for a segment (any grouping of product or location) and viewed the entire system inventory after changes have been made to master data parameters. This allowed me to understand the impact to inventory for any product-location segment that I want to observe.

4. *Spreadsheet:* The spreadsheet contains the actual supply chain planning values that are related to the selected objects, which are chosen to the left. The spreadsheet displays key figures as rows and time buckets as columns. The time buckets are adjustable and set during the initial configuration of the implementation

(http://www.scmfocus.com/sapplanning/2010/02/24/the-storage-buckets-profile-and-the-planning-buckets-profile/).

Each Planning Book can have its own distinct planning buckets, and the planning bucket (day, week, month) can differ depending upon where they are situated on the planning horizon.

(http://www.scmfocus.com/sapplanning/2011/02/17/creating-telescoping-view-in-the-planning-book/)

A planning horizon is how far out the application "sees," or creates recommendations, which may be less than or equal to the planning horizon shown in the Planning Book. I will discuss key figures in detail in the following section.

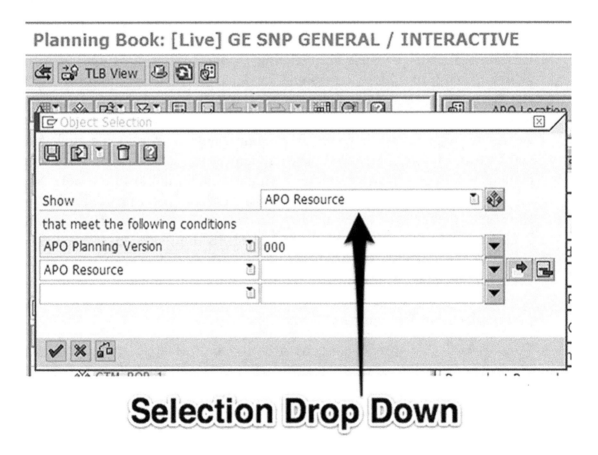

Selection Drop Down

The screen shot above shows how the selection profile is created. There is quite a bit of flexibility in creating selections. The selection options include:

1. *APO Component*
2. *APO Component Assembly*
3. *APO Destination Location*
4. *APO Location*
5. *APO PPM/PDS Name*
6. *APO Product*
7. *APO Resource*
8. *APO Source Location*
9. *APO Transportation Lane*
10. *APO Usage*
11. *APO Usage (Assembly)*
12. *APO Location Product (Header)*
13. *APO Location Product (Member)*
14. *APO Resource (Header)*
15. *APO Resource (Member)*
16. *Interchangeability Group*
17. *Predecessor Location Product*
18. *Successor Location Product*

The number of selection options provides a tremendous amount of flexibility in the view within the Planning Book, but while the selections are created and saved in the Planning Book, they apply equally to how the methods in APO are run. They are in effect fully dual purpose. This dual-purpose nature of the Selection Profile is shown in the following screen shots:

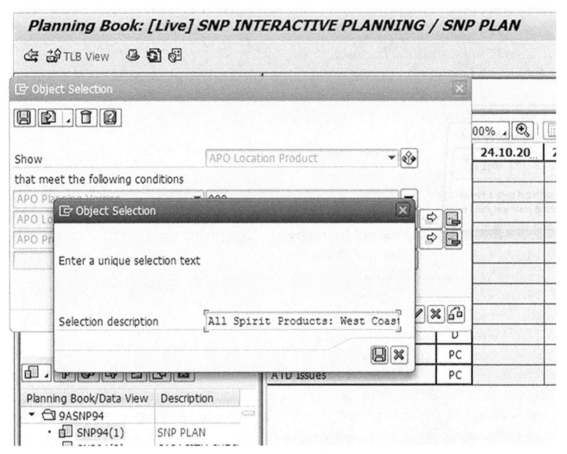

Here I am creating a new Selection Profile within the Planning Book. There is plenty of space, so the Selection Profile can be made quite specific. As the name implies, I have included all spirit products for one region of the US: the West Coast.

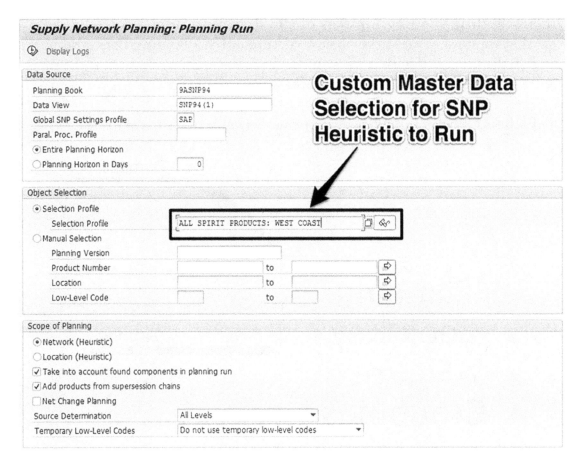

Now I have navigated to the SNP heuristic screen, where the SNP heuristic can be set up as well as run. Notice that instead of entering in the master data for which the SNP heuristic will be applied, I have entered the "All Spirit Products: West Coast," that I created in the Planning Book. In this example, I am showing how to run the SNP heuristic through the SAP user interface (SAPGUI). However, any SNP heuristic variant (profile) can be automatically scheduled, and multiple variants can be scheduled to be run in any sequence.

This is a basic functionality that tends to be underused; there is a tendency to not use the many different selection options that are available in the Planning Book. I will revisit the topic of selection creation when I cover the topic of creating auto adjusting SNP heuristic variants and CTM profiles. Selection creation is not only about how a view is created in the Planning Book, but it also controls how these two supply planning methods are assigned the product-location combinations for processing.

Understanding the Key Figures of the Planning Book
Now that we have covered the basic structure of the Planning Book and how to bring up the information that we want to view, we can move on to how the rows—what SAP calls the "key figures"—work.

The Planning Book's spreadsheet is segmented into three main areas:

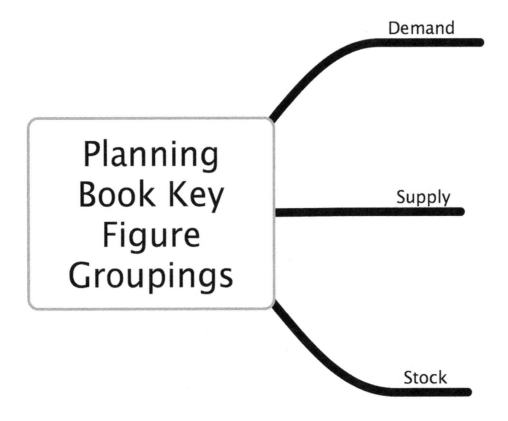

Even though there are key figures in specific areas of the Planning Book that are easily categorized, unfortunately the Planning Book does not have inherent coloration, or any other identifying factor to assist the user to immediately interpret which areas are the demand key figure grouping, the supply key figure grouping, or the stock key figure grouping. However, we can rectify that a bit by showing how the sequence of key figures relates to the logic of the Planning Book.

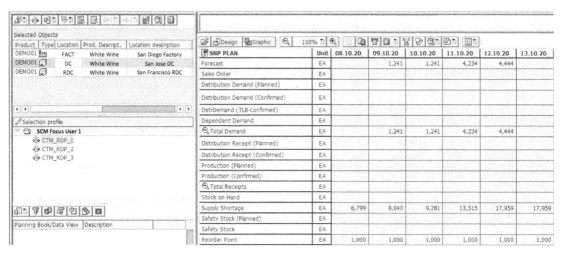

One could logically superimpose boxes over each area, the top box being demand key figures and the lower box being supply key figures, and the bottom being the stock key figures. I have done this graphically on the following page with a mockup of the Planning Book in Excel by adding a vertical tab that identifies each key figure category.

Planning Book Mockup

Key Figure Name	Common Order Categories	10/5/12	10/12/12	10/19/12	10/26/12	11/2/12	11/9/12
Demand Forecast		5,000	1,000	300	400	800	900
Sales Order		5,500	-	-	-	-	-
Distribution Demand	Unconfirmed Purchase Requisition (either internal or external source of supply)			1,200			
Distribution Demand Confirmed	Confirmed Purchase Requisitions or Purchase Orders						
Dependent Demand							
Total Demand		**5,500**	**1,000**	**1,500**	400	800	900
Supply Distribution Receipt	Stock Transport or Purchase Requisition			200			
Distribution Receipt Confirmed	Stock Transport Orders and Purchase Orders						
In Transit		500					
Production Planned		2,800	600	1,300	400	800	900
Production Confirmed							
Total Receipts		**3,300**	**600**	**1,500**	400	800	900
Stock Stock on Hand		1,000	600	600	600	600	600
Max Stock Level		600	600	600	600	600	600
Reorder Point		500	500	500	500	500	500
Safety Stock		500	300	300	300	300	300

This is a mockup of the Planning Book. The key figures listed above are not all the key figures that can appear in the Planning Book, just the most common ones.

There is an inconsistency in the Planning Book in that even internal movements are shown as purchase requisitions in the Distribution Receipt key figure at the receiving location. They are shown this way even though they are in fact stock transport requisitions. However, the same stock transport requisition shows as a stock transport requisition (not a purchase requisition) in the Distribution Demand key figure at the sending location.

Composition of the Key Figures

Each key figure in the Planning Book spreadsheet can be made up of the following items:

1. Standard Order Categories
2. Custom Order Categories
3. Standard Macros
4. Custom Macros

APO ships with a standard set of key figures. These key figures in turn contain a standard set of assigned category groups, which in turn contain order categories. Everyone is familiar with order categories. A purchase requisition and stock transport requisition are both order categories.

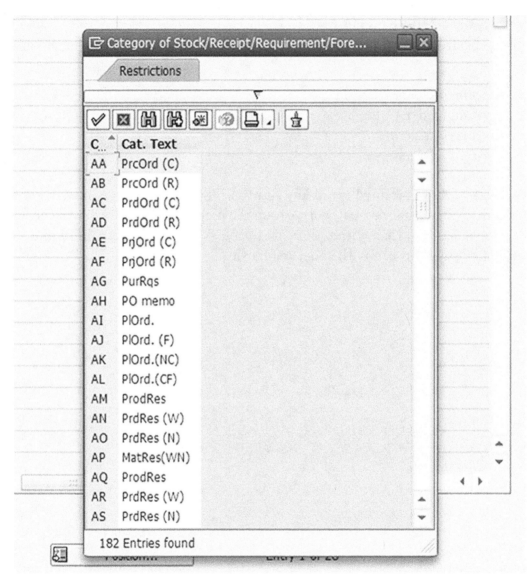

This screen shot shows some of the order categories that ship with SAP APO. Custom order categories can be created, but then there is work in configuring how a custom order category will be treated, in which key figure it will appear, and how it will interact with SAP ERP.

More on this topic is covered in the article below:

http://www.scmfocus.com/sapplanning/2011/06/09/order-and-forecast-categories/

For instance, when an unconfirmed stock transport requisition is created (which occurs during the initial supply plan), APO assigns that order category to specific key figures (actually, to two key figures in this case, but one per product-location combination—Distribution Demand at the sending location and Distribution Receipt at the receiving location). Additionally, all of the order categories can be moved to any of the key figures. When this is performed, then the key figure has been customized.

APO also ships with a set of standard macros. A macro is a formula that has been created in the APO Macro Builder. SAP has created a number of standard formulas that make up the standard macros. The APO Macro Builder allows both for the adjustment of standard macros and the creation of new macros. New macros can be added to new key figures (with the caveat that inserting any key figure above any other key figure with a macro means that that the lower macros must be adjusted; unlike Excel, the Planning Book rows use absolute rather than relative references). Any adjustment to an existing macro or creation of a new macro means the macro is customized.

Up to this point we have discussed what the Planning Book is, how it is structured, and the fact that it is composed of key figures. Key figures are made up of different category groups, which are containers for different order categories and both custom and standard macros. It's now time to talk about how to read the Planning Book and how the planning values "flow" through the Planning Book. We will trace this flow all the way from demand to stock.

Background on the Flow of Requisitions in SNP

SAP SNP has a standard way of displaying and controlling the flow of distribution demand through the supply network. It does this internally by creating new objects in response to precursor objects (for instance, converting demand into distribution demand), and changing the state of the objects' order categories that have already been created (for instance, changing an unconfirmed stock transport requisition into a confirmed stock transport requisition). In the Planning Book, the stock movements show as a series of distribution demands and distribution receipts at each product location, each with their own key figure. A simplified mockup of how this works is shown in the graphic below.

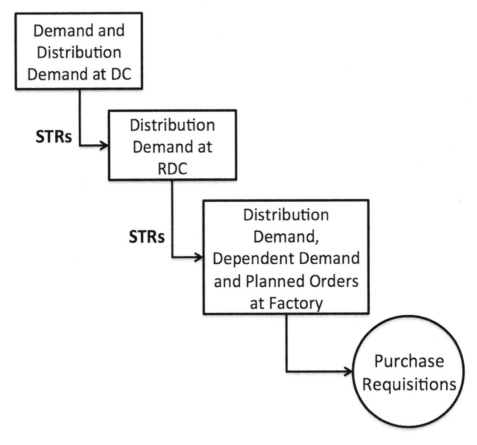

Flow of Demand Through the Supply Network

The Flow of the Supply Network, Order Categories and the Planning Book
For the most part, the movements between facilities are shown as either distribution demand or distribution receipts (two sides of the stock transport requisition).

The exceptions are the very top of the supply network (where the forecast and sales orders are entered for distribution centers), and at the production locations (where dependent demand and planned orders are created) and stock transport requisitions (which appear as shown in the spreadsheet screen shot below).

Movement Types, Ouput and Key Figures in SAP APO

System	Movement Type	Activity	Output	DPA	Key Figure in APO Planning Book
APO	External	Initial Supply Planning Run	Unconfirmed Purchase Req	N/A	Distribution Receipt
APO	External	Deployment Run	Confirmed Purchase Req	N/A	Confirmed Distribution Receipt
APO, ERP	External	TLB or in ERP (standard for vendors, where the APO implementing company does not load build)	Purchase Order	N/A	Confirmed Distribution Receipt
APO	Internal	Initial Supply Planning Run	Unconfirmed Stock Transport Req	No	Distribution Demand
APO	Internal	Deployment Run	Confirmed Stock Transport Req	Yes	Confirmed Distribution Demand
APO, ERP	Internal	TLB	Stock Transport Order	Yes	Confirmed Distribution Demand

Once in ERP, editing of STO or PO is no longer possible in APO. Changes to STO and PO in ERP is reflected in APO.

As can be seen in the screen shot above, SNP has a standard workflow, which starts with unconfirmed requisitions and finishes with orders. All of this can happen (although it's just one option) before the orders are sent over to SAP ERP.

Understanding the Product View

The Product View is probably the second most frequently used view in SNP. Technically it is part of PP/DS. However, I estimate that the Product View is used more by supply planning than production planning and scheduling, regardless of the application in which it is housed.

The Elements Tab

The product view consists of a number of tabs, but we will be focusing on just two. One is the Elements Tab, which is more of an overview of stock movements into and out of a location, in addition to planned orders (if the location is a factory).

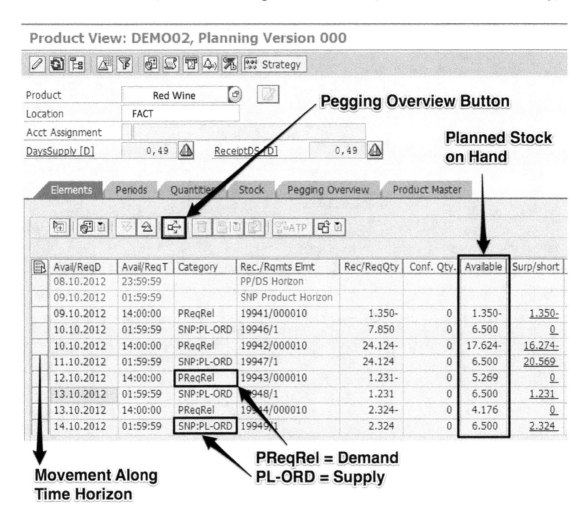

Product View: DEMO02, Planning Version 000

Product	Red Wine		**Pegging Overview Button**
Location	FACT		
Acct Assignment			**Planned Stock**
DaysSupply [D]	0,49 ⚠	ReceiptDS [D]	0,49 ⚠ **on Hand**

Elements Periods Quantities Stock Pegging Overview Product Master

Avail/ReqD	Avail/ReqT	Category	Rec./Rqmts Elmt	Rec/ReqQty	Conf. Qty.	Available	Surp/short
08.10.2012	23:59:59		PP/DS Horizon				
09.10.2012	01:59:59		SNP Product Horizon				
09.10.2012	14:00:00	PReqRel	19941/000010	1.350-	0	1.350-	1.350-
10.10.2012	01:59:59	SNP:PL-ORD	19946/1	7.850	0	6.500	0
10.10.2012	14:00:00	PReqRel	19942/000010	24.124-	0	17.624-	16.274-
11.10.2012	01:59:59	SNP:PL-ORD	19947/1	24.124	0	6.500	20.569
12.10.2012	14:00:00	PReqRel	19943/000010	1.231-	0	5.269	0
13.10.2012	01:59:59	SNP:PL-ORD	948/1	1.231	0	6.500	1.231
13.10.2012	14:00:00	PReqRel	19944/000010	2.324-	0	4.176	0
14.10.2012	01:59:59	SNP:PL-ORD	19949/1	2.324	0	6.500	2.324

Movement Along Time Horizon

PReqRel = Demand
PL-ORD = Supply

The Elements Tab of the Product View provides quite a different view into a product location than does the Planning Book. First, the Product View can only look at one product location at a time. Unlike the Planning Book, the Product View can only show a product-location combination and has none of the ability to customize the selections created; in fact, the Product View cannot create any selections. However, it is still very useful and can be used to show pegging (albeit less definitively and with much less detail than the Pegging Overview Tab), as well as show different views of the movements into and out of a product location. The pegging that is shown in the Elements Tab is per supply and demand element. However, the Pegging Overview will show the pegging all the way through the supply network, from initial demand to either a planned order or a purchase requisition, if these peggings exist in the system. This can be found for a specific line item in the Elements Tab by selecting the line item and then selecting the Pegging button.

The Pegging Overview
Peggings were explained in Chapter 3: "Combining Supply Methods Across External Planning Systems and ERP Systems," so I won't describe them again here. My primary reason for going into the Product View is to demonstrate the peggings that are created by our different methods, and the effect of the final pegging that we run at the end of each test.

Now that we have reviewed the Planning Book and the Product View (how we will observe the output of the various planning methods that we select), the setup of each test is the topic of the next chapter.

Conclusion
This chapter was designed to provide you with all the necessary background in order to properly interpret the next chapter. In this chapter, I explained the following:

1. Prototyping is important as it provides the detailed and accurate information about how the system behaves under different configurations and settings.
2. A demo map is a useful tool for helping to set up what is to be tested, and to demonstrate to an audience what is being shown by helping them to follow the system. Supply planning can be challenging to demonstrate because it requires that you move continually among different locations (typically for one product). As a result, it can be confusing for the audience to understand what product location the system is displaying. The demo map is just one of the documentation tools necessary to properly explain and provide

transparency of testing and the evolution of the design to those outside of the module implementation team.

3. While a number of foundational tasks are necessary to create an APO model, this chapter has focused on the setup of the methods and the fields in the product-location master, some of which are the method modifiers. These are the most germane settings that relate to the multi method approach prototype, which is demonstrated in the following chapter.

4. To me, a best practice of implementation is to mock up the configuration and product-location master, as well as foundational configuration data, into a spreadsheet prior to setting up a prototype in APO (or any other supply planning application for that matter). This Excel file becomes a way of getting to common agreement as to what will be prototyped (and eventually set up in the final configuration), as well as documentation of the model.

5. This chapter covered the settings related to the methods and the product-location master fields, which are used to control the prototype in the following chapter.

6. I described the basic setup of the prototype, including its supply network, methods and method modifiers. The model shown was adequate to test the hypothesis that multiple supply planning methods and modifiers could be made to work together. Prototypes tend to start out small and basic; more and more are added to prototypes as new hypotheses need to be tested.

7. In this chapter, the different areas of the Planning Book, its key figures, macros, category groups, order categories were covered, in addition to how data flows through the key figures in the Planning Book.

8. The chapter concluded by explaining the Product View, which is the second most popular user interface among supply planners and serves several purposes, including a way to view peggings.

CHAPTER 5

Prototyping the Multi Method Supply Planning Model

Understanding Prototyping

Wikipedia has the following definition of a prototype:

> *A prototype is an early sample or model built to test a concept or process or to act as a thing to be replicated or learned from. It is a term used in a variety of contexts, including semantics, design, electronics, and software programming. A prototype is designed to test and trial a new design to enhance precision by system analysts and users. Prototyping serves to provide specifications for a real, working system rather than a theoretical one.*

The word prototype derives from the Greek (prototypon), "primitive form"

> *In general, an iterative series of prototypes will be designed, constructed and tested as the final design emerges and is prepared for production. With rare*

exceptions, multiple iterations of prototypes are used to progressively refine the design. A common strategy is to design, test, evaluate and then modify the design based on analysis of the prototype.

— Wikipedia

The more complex the model, the more important it is to work with a "primitive form." However, prototypes are helpful for a wide variety of circumstances and applications. Complex systems cannot generally be communicated in their entirety—along with all their implications—through presentations and oral and written communication. This is where prototyping comes in.

The best way to understand a prototype is to understand how it differs from a production system. While the differences between prototyping and production design listed below are from the product design perspective, the description is applicable to software prototyping as well.

- *Materials:* Production materials may require manufacturing processes involving higher capital costs than what is practical for prototyping. Instead, engineers or prototyping specialists will attempt to substitute materials with properties that simulate the intended final material.

- *Processes:* Often expensive and time-consuming unique tooling is required to fabricate a custom design. Prototypes will often compromise by using more flexible processes. Final production designs often require extensive effort to capture high-volume manufacturing detail. Such detail is generally unwarranted for prototypes as some refinement to the design is to be expected. Often prototypes are built using very limited engineering detail as compared to the final production intent.

A prototype, therefore, allows concepts to be tested at a lower cost and with more flexibility and speed. For instance, automobiles are initially designed and reviewed on a computer or in clay before they are fashioned in metal. When a prototype is built, it may not be built with the final materials that will be used in the production item. However, by creating a reasonable semblance of what the final product will look like, the designers can take input and make changes.

I am an advocate of prototyping, as the following articles can attest. I have performed prototyping in demand planning, supply planning and production planning software, and in different vendor applications. The basic process works the same across all supply chain planning applications.

http://www.scmfocus.com/supplychainsimulation/2012/05/27/mrp-drp-prototyping-external-systems/

While accepted in many other areas, prototyping in general does not get the respect that it deserves in IT. In fact, prototyping is often de-emphasized on some projects with the excuse that the project timelines do not allow for it, which is akin to saying: "There was not time allocated on the project for a quality implementation." Imagine if Ford told its customers that in order to reduce their time to market, they had decided to skip the prototyping phase? Who would want such a car, which had been designed with such a low quality approach? Considering the high failure rate of enterprise software projects, skipping steps in the process that would improve quality—such as prototyping—would seem an obvious thing to avoid.

My experience is that when prototyping is skipped on a project, much more time is spent repairing design and configuration mistakes than if prototyping had been done in the first place. All projects seem to waste a number of months as they begin to gather the business requirements, so this is the time to begin prototyping—early and often. The major consulting companies tend not to perform prototyping and I have not determined whether they just don't really understand effective system implementation, or if this approach in some way maximizes their billing hours by lengthening the project duration.

Focus On  The Partner Structure at the Large Consulting Companies

That large IT consulting companies don't know how to implement enterprise software may seem a strange contention; nonetheless, all of my experience supports this conclusion. An analysis of the institutional structure and the internal incentives at large consulting companies provides insight as to why.

In large consulting companies, glorified salesmen are called "partners." They are in their positions because of their ability to sell. Partners have very high demands placed on them to sell. I believe the services sales quota for a partner of any of the large consulting companies in the US is roughly $2 million per year. An experienced partner will take in roughly $500,000 per year for meeting this sales quota, meaning that they are commissioned salesmen with a twenty-five percent commission. Selling consulting services is far more lucrative than actually doing consulting work, with a full-time consultant getting roughly one third of their billing rate and an independent consultant getting roughly one half. The more sales you bring in, the bigger your say in all aspects of how the company does business (very senior partners can make $2 million in salary per year). Partner level resources—often called "directors" to differentiate them from partners because they cannot sell—are focused on implementation. However, their status within the companies is considerably lower than that of partners and they don't set the policy of the company. Therefore, individuals with these types of sales demands on them are not particularly focused on implementation quality or learning from past implementations. They must maintain that $2 million sales quota. Two years in a row of missing the quota typically results in them being asked to leave the consulting company. There is an enormous amount of money in selling consulting services, more than there is in actually doing the consulting work itself.

http://www.scmfocus.com/sapprojectmanagement/2010/06/what-percentage-of-the-hourly-rate-is-taken-by-the-partner/

As a consequence, there is no lie that consulting companies won't tell to get a contract, as is demonstrated by this article, which provides insights gleaned from court documents into sales practices:

http://www.scmfocus.com/sapprojectmanagement/2012/02/deloittes-puffery-in-their-rfp-to-marin-county-and-what-it-means-for-current-and-future-clients/

In their desire to win business, many consulting companies go beyond lying (i.e., what the courts call "puffery") and into bribery. In the Marin County case, Deloitte bribed an individual with auditing oversight of their work, which is interesting because Deloitte is also an auditing organization (they have both consulting and auditing arms). However, the major consulting/auditing companies in the country are part of every financial crisis—from the dot.com bubble to the housing crisis. Therefore, the major consulting firms that have audit divisions both bribe—and are bribed as a normal course of business (the bribe often takes the form of a company buying "more" consulting services in return for consideration on auditing leniency as was the case at Enron).

http://www.scmfocus.com/sapprojectmanagement/2012/02/has-deloitte-bought-off-someone-inside-your-organization-as-they-did-with-marin-county/

Prototyping Post Go-Live

One more topic I would like to bring up before leaving this high-level examination of prototyping is that prototyping is not only applicable to the implementation stage. Although it is the type of prototyping I discuss in this book, prototyping is also very useful for troubleshooting live implementations of software that is not meeting expectations, or for simply attempting to improve any application. This type of prototyping can sometimes mean building a small model in the same application that is being used. However, other times it can mean getting a second application with a very similar set of functionality and comparing the output of an application.[4]

I have used external prototype environments very successfully to troubleshoot SAP DP implementations. Very rarely does SAP DP software implement cleanly, and in most cases it will have multiple issues ranging from technical missteps related to the configuration of the software, to the basic functioning of things such as best fit and disaggregation, to users rejecting the DP interface. These types of issues require an external forecasting prototype environment. I proposed in the

---

[4] This is nowhere as expensive as it sounds. Depending upon the supply chain software area, there can be a number of reasonably priced alternatives, particularly if one purchases "simulation" versions of the application.

book, *Supply Planning with MRP, DRP and APS Software,* that external cost optimizers be used to validate and prototype the SNP cost optimizer.

The following articles describe how to use prototype environments for several different purposes:

http://www.scmfocus.com/sapplanning/2011/10/12/using-an-external-system-to-check-optimization-results/

http://www.scmfocus.com/demandplanning/2010/07/prototype-environment-and-background/

Finally...the Actual Prototype Testing

It took some time to cover the foundational material necessary to put us into a position to go through the prototype test, but we have finally arrived.

The Prototype Design

This chapter will show the output of three real scenarios that were tested. Each scenario has a different combination of planning methods that are used to plan a three-echelon supply network. As discussed earlier, once three echelons can be planned, it is a straightforward matter to extend the concept to more echelons, which is in fact what I did for a company after this test was completed.

Products

Location	White Wine	Red Wine	Zinfandel	Run Sequence
San Jose DC	CTM	CTM	Target Days' Supply	1. CTM for White Wine & Red Wine 2. Heuristic for Zinfandel
San Francisco RDC	CTM	Target Stocking Level	CTM	3. CTM for White Wine & Zinfandel 4. Heuristic for Red Wine
San Diego Factory (Bottling)	Target Days' Supply	CTM	CTM	5. CTM for White Wine 6. Heuristic for Zinfandel
BOM	Wine, Cork, Bottle Label	Wine, Cork, Bottle Label	Wine, Cork, Bottle Label	
Napa Winery	Unmodified Heuristic	Reorder Point w/ forecast	Reorder Point w/o forecast	7. Heuristic for All
San Diego Winery	Unmodified Heuristic	Unmodified Heuristic	Unmodified Heuristic	8. Heuristic for All

This graphic shows the planning run logic of the demo. It shows the master data of the demo, as well as the setup of the profiles for CTM and the SNP heuristic and their sequence. The run sequence of the different methods changes depending upon what method is used for the top of the supply network. It is important to chart out what is to be tested prior to actually making the configuration changes. Doing so helps to keep the configuration clear among the multiple people working on a team, but is also useful if only one person is doing all of the work. However, regardless of who does the work, eventually the logic will have to be explained to the business, and this same spreadsheet, or similar organizational document, is useful for both explaining the test, as well as documenting the multiple versions or changes to the configuration. This branches into the topic of simulation, as simulation is defined as the alteration of a copy of the model, running the application, and then documenting the results.

Each test is identified by what is being tested. The hypothetical company is *ZYX Wine Distribution*. The three locations are:

1. San Jose Distribution Center
2. San Francisco Regional Distribution Center
3. San Diego Factory

The three products are:

1. White Wine
2. Red Wine
3. Zinfandel

Each test is introduced by a heading that explains the methods and method modifiers applied to each product-location combination.

One thing I wanted to discuss before we get into the many screen shots in this chapter is the issue of SAP displaying periods instead of commas in the Product View. This is the European number setting. So what would be the number 4,342 for an American would be 4.342 for a European. These screen shots were taken from a European APO instance, so my User Profile was set as a European. I could have easily changed what is referred to as the decimal notation, because the setting is actually in the User Profile—therefore it can be adjusted per user. I have a screen shot of the User Profile where the decimal notation is located on the following page:

However, after working with the European settings for a while I had simply become used to it that I did not change the setting.

Your will also notice that the decimal notation in the Planning Book is with a comma so 4,342. This is because, interestingly, changing the User Profile to the European decimal notation does not affect the Planning Book and there is no way to change it to European decimal notation in the Planning Book or anywhere else. This is discussed in the thread below:

http://scn.sap.com/thread/1241945

I have taken the liberty on the Product View screen shots to use the American decimal notation of 4,324 when I have performed markup in the hopes of clarifying that most the screen shots are dealing in 000s.

Test One: Run Sequence DC—Target Days' Supply, RDC—CTM, Factory—Unmodified SNP Heuristic

This test seeks to determine whether the first sequence described in the spreadsheet above is a workable solution. The first step of the test is to view the San Jose distribution center. We will begin with the product "White Wine" at the three locations.

The Planning Book Before Step One:

Here we have a forecast (which has been released to SNP by DP), but we have no Distribution Receipt. As nothing has been run yet, we would not expect the rest of the Planning Book to be populated with values. This will change as soon as we run the SNP heuristic on this product-location combination.

SNP PLAN	Unit	08.10.20	09.10.20	10.10.20	11.10.20	12.10.20	13.10.20
Forecast	EA		1,241	1,241	4,234	4,444	
Sales Order	EA						
Distribution Demand (Planned)	EA						
Distribution Demand (Confirmed)	EA						
DistrDemand (TLB-Confirmed)	EA						
Dependent Demand	EA						
Total Demand	EA		1,241	1,241	4,234	4,444	
Distribution Receipt (Planned)	EA						
Distribution Receipt (Confirmed)	EA						
Production (Planned)	EA						
Production (Confirmed)	EA						
Total Receipts	EA						
Stock on Hand	EA						
Supply Shortage	EA	6,799	8,040	9,281	13,515	17,959	17,959
Safety Stock (Planned)	EA						
Safety Stock	EA						
Reorder Point	EA	1,000	1,000	1,000	1,000	1,000	1,000

Selected Objects:

Product	Type	Location	Prod. Descript.	Location description
DEMO01	FACT	White Wine	San Diego Factory	
DEMO01	DC	White Wine	San Jose DC	
DEMO01	RDC	White Wine	San Francisco RDC	

Selection profile
SCM Focus User 1
- CTM_ROP_1
- CTM_ROP_2
- CTM_ROP_3

Planning Book/Data View   Description

We can already see that the reorder point of 1000 appears in the Reorder Point key figure. No supply planning methods have yet been run, so SNP has not populated the Planning Book with planned values.

Now we will run the SNP heuristic. On the following page is the variant, or profile, that shows the setting for which the heuristic will run.

Supply Network Planning: Planning Run

⏱ 🔁 Display Logs

Data Source

Planning Book	9ASNP94
Data View	SNP94(1)
Global SNP Settings Profile	SAP
Paral. Proc. Profile	

◉ Entire Planning Horizon
○ Planning Horizon in Days   0

Object Selection

○ Selection Profile

Selection Profile ⟋

◉ Manual Selection

Planning Version	000
Product Number	Red Wine to
Location	San Jose DC to
Low-Level Code	to

Scope of Planning

◉ Network (Heuristic)
○ Location (Heuristic)
☑ Take into account found components in planning run
☑ Add products from supersession chains
☐ Net Change Planning

Source Determination	All Levels
Temporary Low-Level Codes	Do not use temporary low-level codes

The heuristic variant is used to save settings that can be re run. SNP can save any number of heuristic variants. A process chain can be used to trigger various SNP heuristic variants, or any other methods profile in SNP. These profiles and variants are typically controlled by a batch job after the system is live.

SNP PLAN	Unit	08.10.20	09.10.20	10.10.20	11.10.20	12.10.20	13.10.20
Forecast	EA		1,241	1,241	4,234	4,444	
Sales Order	EA						
Distribution Demand (Planned)	EA						
Distribution Demand (Confirmed)	EA						
DistrDemand (TLB-Confirmed)	EA						
Dependent Demand	EA						
Total Demand	EA		1,241	1,241	4,234	4,444	
Distribution Receipt (Planned)	EA	8,299	1,241	1,241	4,234	4,444	
Distribution Receipt (Confirmed)	EA						
Production (Planned)	EA						
Production (Confirmed)	EA						
Total Receipts	EA	8,299	1,241	1,241	4,234	4,444	
Stock on Hand	EA	1,500	1,500	1,500	1,500	1,500	1,500
Supply Shortage	EA						
Safety Stock (Planned)	EA						
Safety Stock	EA						
Reorder Point	EA	1,000	1,000	1,000	1,000	1,000	1,000
Target Days' Supply	D						

Selected Objects

Product	Type	Location	Prod. Descript.	Location description
DEMO01		FACT	White Wine	San Diego Factory
DEMO01		DC	White Wine	San Jose DC
DEMO01		RDC	White Wine	San Francisco RDC

Selection profile
SCM Focus User 1
  CTM_ROP_1
  CTM_ROP_2
  CTM_ROP_3

Planning Book/Data View | Description

After the SNP heuristic, we now have values populating the Distribution Receipt key figure. This is an unconfirmed stock transport requisition, which is sourced from the San Francisco RDC. It is possible to set up multi sourcing in SNP, which can be controlled with a priority or a quota arrangement (if the SNP heuristic is used). However, because this model is single-sourced at each location, any stock transport requisition can only come from the San Francisco RDC. Quota arrangements are discussed in the following post:

http://www.scmfocus.com/sapplanning/2008/09/14/quota-arrangements-in-scm/

Additionally, the SNP heuristic respected the reorder point and in essence carried extra stock in order to meet the reorder point requirement. This is a rule that generalizes. When the SNP heuristic is run in an unmodified form (no reorder points, target days' supply, etc.), the method is very much a "pull" approach: it reacts by placing inventory into the supply network when there is demand. However, when the SNP heuristic is run in a modified form, the method then places stock into the supply network ahead of demand. In this way, the method becomes a "push" approach. The larger the modification to the SNP heuristic (the greater the days' supply, the higher the reorder points) the method moves more toward the push end of the continuum. Looked at another way, the larger the modifications, the less the demand drives the inventory trigger, and vice versa. While the SNP heuristic or MRP in ERP systems is generally criticized as overly simplistic, if the modification values are calculated with significant intelligence, as is described in the section of this chapter on inventory optimization and multi echelon planning, both the SNP heuristic and MRP can become considerably more intelligent.[5]

SNP PLAN	Unit	08.10.20	09.10.20	10.10.20	11.10.20	12.10.20	13.10.20
Forecast	EA						
Sales Order	EA						
Distribution Demand (Planned)	EA	8,299	1,241	1,241	4,234	4,444	
Distribution Demand (Confirmed)	EA						
DistrDemand (TLB-Confirmed)	EA						
Dependent Demand	EA						
Total Demand	EA	8,299	1,241	1,241	4,234	4,444	
Distribution Receipt (Planned)	EA						
Distribution Receipt (Confirmed)	EA						
Production (Planned)	EA						
Production (Confirmed)	EA						
Total Receipts	EA						
Stock on Hand	EA						
Supply Shortage	EA	8,299	9,540	10,781	15,015	19,459	19,459

Selected Objects

Product	Type	Location	Prod. Descript.	Location description
DEMO01		FACT	White Wine	San Diego Factory
DEMO01		DC	White Wine	San Jose DC
DEMO01		RDC	White Wine	San Francisco RDC

Selection profile
▽ SCM Focus User 1
 CTM_ROP_1
 CTM_ROP_2
 CTM_ROP_3

Here we can see the exact same quantities in the Distribution Demand key figure of the Planning Book for the product-location combination of White Wine at the San Francisco RDC. These stock transport requisitions have been created out in time. While there are no values in the Distribution Receipt key figure, this will be populated after we run the CTM Profile that we have created for this test.

In the screen shot on the following page, we can see that CTM has populated the Distribution Receipt.

---

[5] Regarding the specific modifier of the reorder point, in the book *Supply Planning with MRP, DRP and APS Software,* I talk about how reorder points are unfairly maligned for lacking sophistication and visibility. However, anyone who has followed the academic literature on reorder points would find that reorder point calculation methods can be quite sophisticated (although industry does tend to use simple reorder point development methods based more on trial and error), and reorder points are sometimes made to forward calculate. For instance, SNP's reorder points forward calculate as was described in Chapter 2: "The Concept Behind Combined Supply Planning Methods." In my book on supply planning, I draw the distinction between using forecast-based methods for supply planning and non forecast-based methods (such as the traditional/no forward calculation reorder point). A forecastability formula could be used to determine which products should be placed on forecast-based methods or non forecast-based methods. However, the development of forward-based calculation reorder points makes the decision matrix that one would use for method assignment to a product location more complex than ever.

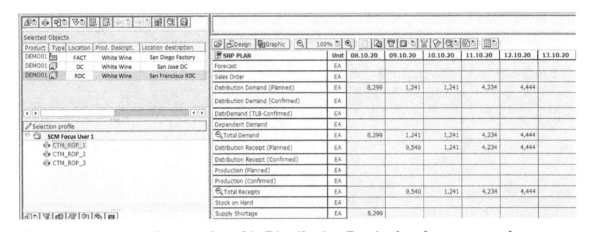

SNP PLAN	Unit	08.10.20	09.10.20	10.10.20	11.10.20	12.10.20	13.10.20
Forecast	EA						
Sales Order	EA						
Distribution Demand (Planned)	EA	8,299	1,241	1,241	4,234	4,444	
Distribution Demand (Confirmed)	EA						
DistrDemand (TLB-Confirmed)	EA						
Dependent Demand	EA						
Total Demand	EA	8,299	1,241	1,241	4,234	4,444	
Distribution Receipt (Planned)	EA		9,540	1,241	4,234	4,444	
Distribution Receipt (Confirmed)	EA						
Production (Planned)	EA						
Production (Confirmed)	EA						
Total Receipts	EA		9,540	1,241	4,234	4,444	
Stock on Hand	EA						
Supply Shortage	EA	8,299					

The order categories that populate this Distribution Receipt key figure are stock transport requisitions. The source of supply for these stock transport requisitions is the San Diego Factory. Therefore, CTM has successfully planned the second echelon in this supply network.

When we check the Planning Book for the San Diego Factory, we will see the newly-created Distribution Demand. However, we will now want to plan the final echelon, the San Diego Factory, by running the SNP heuristic.

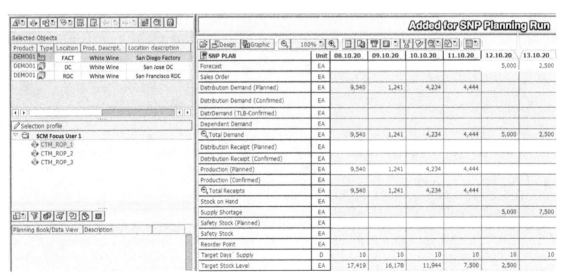

Added for SNP Planning Run

SNP PLAN	Unit	08.10.20	09.10.20	10.10.20	11.10.20	12.10.20	13.10.20
Forecast	EA					5,000	2,500
Sales Order	EA						
Distribution Demand (Planned)	EA	9,540	1,241	4,234	4,444		
Distribution Demand (Confirmed)	EA						
DistrDemand (TLB-Confirmed)	EA						
Dependent Demand	EA						
Total Demand	EA	9,540	1,241	4,234	4,444	5,000	2,500
Distribution Receipt (Planned)	EA						
Distribution Receipt (Confirmed)	EA						
Production (Planned)	EA	9,540	1,241	4,234	4,444		
Production (Confirmed)	EA						
Total Receipts	EA	9,540	1,241	4,234	4,444		
Stock on Hand	EA						
Supply Shortage	EA					5,000	7,500
Safety Stock (Planned)	EA						
Safety Stock	EA						
Reorder Point	EA						
Target Days' Supply	D	10	10	10	10	10	10
Target Stock Level	EA	17,419	16,178	11,944	7,500	2,500	

This Planning Book has a lot going on thus far. So let us examine each important area one at a time.

1. *There is the Distribution Demand at the San Diego Factory from stock transport requisitions created between the San Diego Factory and the San Francisco RDC.*
2. *We also have planning production created in order to satisfy this demand.*
3. *After the SNP heuristic ran, I entered a forecast directly onto the factory. In this hypothetical model, the company both satisfies demand from its DCs, but also sells to other distributors directly from its factory. The product leaves the supply network directly from the factory, so this is where the forecast is placed.*

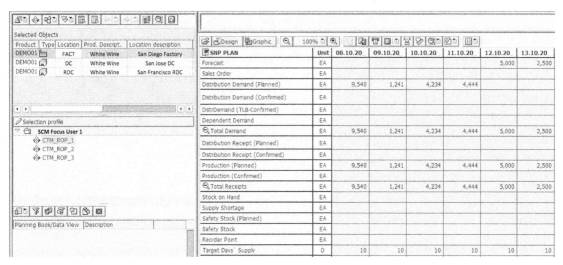

The SNP heuristic is then run again. It can be observed that SNP has now scheduled production in order to meet that demand as well as the distribution demand that was already in the Planning Book. In this particular circumstance, the SNP heuristic could have been run interactively from within the Planning Book, rather than from the SNP heuristic transaction. There are several SNP heuristic run buttons right within the Planning Book.

This leads into a topic that often arises: Can planners re run the SNP heuristic or other methods interactively? When the SNP heuristic is used for the entire supply network, the answer is "yes," but when multiple methods are employed, the answer is far less clear, and in many cases while the SNP heuristic "can" be re run, there are interdependencies *to consider. As this topic is tangential to this book, I have included the following links that cover it in detail:*

http://www.scmfocus.com/sapplanning/2011/12/20/running-the-optimizer-for-a-single-location-versus-the-sub-problem/

http://www.scmfocus.com/sapplanning/2012/06/19/should-ctm-be-run-daily-or-interactively/

The Pegging Run

We have successfully populated the Planning Book with planned values through a three-echelon supply network, with each echelon being planned by a different method. However, this is not the end of the process. Using different supply planning methods will not result in a logical pegging throughout the network, as demonstrated in the Pegging Overview screen shot below:

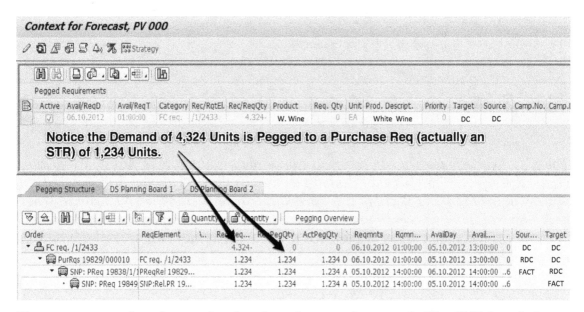

Here we can see that the pegging has been incorrectly created. The SNP heuristic can often result in incorrect peggings. Extensive reviews of peggings created by SNP heuristic show that they are not reliable. In fact, one of the outcomes of this testing was that a final CTM pegging run is in fact necessary to properly align the supplies generated from the heuristic. What was not tested, but would be of some interest, is if CTM could also be

used in a similar way to create the peggings for supplies created by the SNP optimizer. The SAP documentation soft-peddles the benefits of pegging in CTM versus the SNP heuristic or the cost optimizer. CTM simply excels at creating peggings. Furthermore, what is both not covered by SAP documentation as well as other online or book sources is that CTM can be used for pegging of existing supply and demand elements regardless of whether CTM is actually used to create supply elements in response to a demand element.

This conclusion, which was only found through testing and a fortuitous turn of events, is valuable for a number of reasons. It allows both methods (heuristics and the optimizer) to inherit the fixed pegging capability that only CTM has, and allows any company running any supply planning method to create very effective peggings.

The Pegging Relationship Explained

The first pegging (San Francisco RDC to the San Jose RDC) created by the SNP heuristic is really an illogical pegging (the logic here seems to be first in, first out).[6] Another pegging view showed that a forecast for 1,234 units was pegged to a purchase requisition for 4,324 units. There were no capacity constraints in the system (in fact, the SNP heuristic cannot take into account capacity constraints even if they existed). Therefore, the pegging is between the forecast and the initial PurRqs (which are actually stock transfers. The fact that they show as the order PurRqs order category is another bug in SNP). This design is, in my opinion, related to the fact that stock transport requisitions are also technically purchase requisitions. This harkens back to the initial design of SAP ERP when stock transport requisitions were set up as purchase requisitions—but purchase requisitions placed upon internal locations. However, APO will show the same requisition as either a purchase requisition or a stock transport requisition depending upon whether the location is the sender or the recipient of the stock transport requisition. For instance, when one displays the detailed view on the Distribution Receipt key figure, purchase requisitions will often be the order category type "AG." Each key figure contains a series of order categories that, as described in Chapter 4: "Preparing for the Prototype," have been pre-assigned by SAP.

---

[6] Notice that the quantities do not match. The forecast is for 4,324 units, however the pegged quantity is for 1,234 units. This does appear to be 4.324 units and 1.234 units. The decimal is confusing and should be a comma. This is a setting that can be changed in APO; the decimal should be read as a comma.

Now we will look at the exact same product location after the final CTM pegging run has been performed. This is a CTM run that does not create any requisitions or planned orders, but will peg demands and supplies throughout the supply network regardless of what method created the pegging.

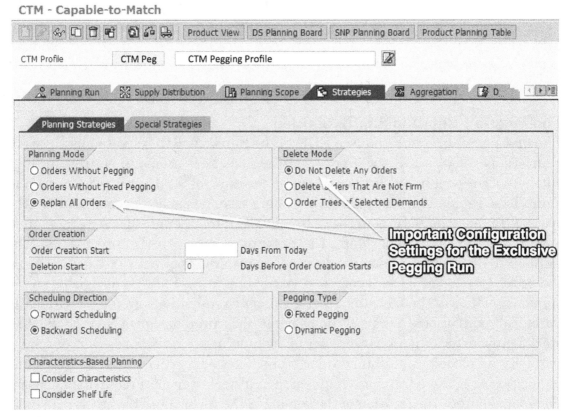

The two important options here are "Replan all Orders" and "Do Not Delete Any Orders." This combination can be made to result in a repegging of all existing supply and demand elements in the supply network. The result is not what the settings would lead you to expect based upon their description, but it is in fact how they work.

This pegging run proved so valuable that we agreed that whenever methods other than CTM are used, the final pegging run should be run. The final pegging run has the benefit of not altering any of the previous recommendations, while simply "connecting the dots" in a very easy-to-manage way. This result is clear in the following screen shot:

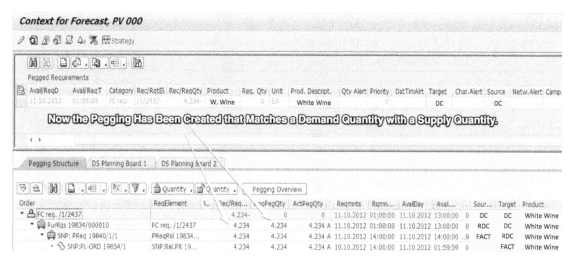

Here we can see that the peggings have been changed, and the supply and demand quantity match one another. The supply that was created in response to the demand is pegged to it.

However, when the same requisition shows as a stock transport requisition, it is viewed in the Distribution Demand key figure in the receiving location and it no longer shows as a purchase requisition but as a stock transport requisition. Because the pegging is being reviewed from the forecast down, purchase requisitions (SNP: Preq) are displayed. If the peggings were viewed from the bottom of the supply network, pegging up to demand, the requisitions would be identified as SNP: Stock Transport Reqs. Therefore, when one is viewing purchase requisitions in the Planning Book that are actually between internal locations, it is necessary to convert that mentally to a stock transport requisition.

Bugs Bugs Bugs

All of these little bugs make the Pegging Overview difficult for first time or infrequent users to benefit from the user interface. A frequent comment made by SAP—as well as executives within the company who need to defend their previous decisions to buy SAP (but who never have to actually touch an SAP user interface)—is that the users need more training or are not using the system properly. However, the examples that I have listed below show how the interface provided by SAP can be incorrect. This is another reason as to why extracting the peggings from SNP and having the planners use an external report can be so valuable.

Errors in the pegging interface that are longstanding and unlikely to be fixed can be rectified in the custom report. A company that had such a report would probably never need its planners to use the flawed pegging view in SAP, which would lead to higher planner productivity as well as a better quality plan.

Conclusion for Test One

As with all of the tests, there was some adjustment required here and there; however, this test was a success both in terms of the planning output created and the detailed pegging that we created. This was the first test of multiple methods, and from here we move on to the second demo test.

Test Two: Run Sequence: DC—CTM, RDC—Reorder Point, Factory—Target Stock Level

This next test is similar to the first, except the methods that plan each echelon have been changed around. The concept behind this is to test multiple methods per echelon to see if any problems are encountered.

The Planning Book Before Step One:

Here we have a forecast (which has been released to SNP by DP), but as with the first test, we have no Distribution Receipt. As no planning methods have yet been run, we would not expect that the rest of the Planning Book be populated with values. However, this will change as we run CTM instead of the SNP heuristic on this product-location combination.

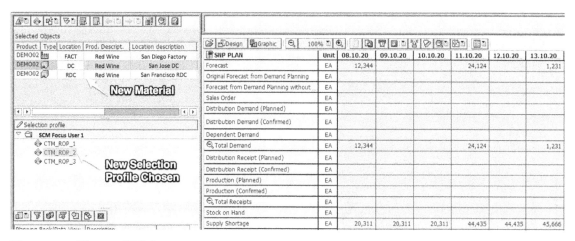

SNP PLAN	Unit	08.10.20	09.10.20	10.10.20	11.10.20	12.10.20	13.10.20
Forecast	EA	12,344			24,124		1,231
Original Forecast from Demand Planning	EA						
Forecast from Demand Planning without	EA						
Sales Order	EA						
Distribution Demand (Planned)	EA						
Distribution Demand (Confirmed)	EA						
Dependent Demand	EA						
Total Demand	EA	12,344			24,124		1,231
Distribution Receipt (Planned)	EA						
Distribution Receipt (Confirmed)	EA						
Production (Planned)	EA						
Production (Confirmed)	EA						
Total Receipts	EA						
Stock on Hand	EA						
Supply Shortage	EA	20,311	20,311	20,311	44,435	44,435	45,666

Now we will run CTM.

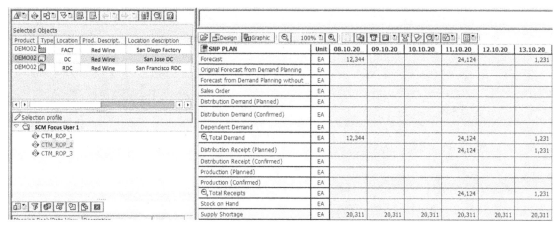

SNP PLAN	Unit	08.10.20	09.10.20	10.10.20	11.10.20	12.10.20	13.10.20
Forecast	EA	12,344			24,124		1,231
Original Forecast from Demand Planning	EA						
Forecast from Demand Planning without	EA						
Sales Order	EA						
Distribution Demand (Planned)	EA						
Distribution Demand (Confirmed)	EA						
Dependent Demand	EA						
Total Demand	EA	12,344			24,124		1,231
Distribution Receipt (Planned)	EA				24,124		1,231
Distribution Receipt (Confirmed)	EA						
Production (Planned)	EA						
Production (Confirmed)	EA						
Total Receipts	EA				24,124		1,231
Stock on Hand	EA						
Supply Shortage	EA	20,311	20,311	20,311	20,311	20,311	20,311

CTM has planned the values for the Distribution Receipt, which again, is composed of stock transport requisitions to the San Francisco RDC.

Next we need to plan the San Francisco RDC, which will be planned with a reorder point.

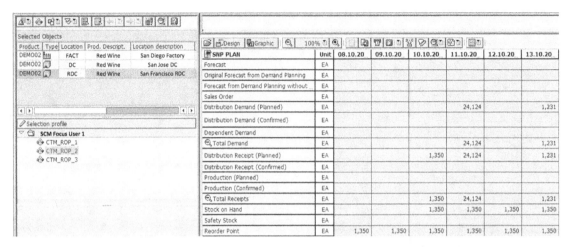

SNP PLAN	Unit	08.10.20	09.10.20	10.10.20	11.10.20	12.10.20	13.10.20
Forecast	EA						
Original Forecast from Demand Planning	EA						
Forecast from Demand Planning without	EA						
Sales Order	EA						
Distribution Demand (Planned)	EA				24,124		1,231
Distribution Demand (Confirmed)	EA						
Dependent Demand	EA						
Total Demand	EA				24,124		1,231
Distribution Receipt (Planned)	EA			1,350	24,124		1,231
Distribution Receipt (Confirmed)	EA						
Production (Planned)	EA						
Production (Confirmed)	EA						
Total Receipts	EA			1,350	24,124		1,231
Stock on Hand	EA			1,350	1,350	1,350	1,350
Safety Stock	EA						
Reorder Point	EA	1,350	1,350	1,350	1,350	1,350	1,350

The reorder point that was entered in the product-location master is 1,350 units. As can be seen above, the reorder point macro calculated the reorder point for each planning bucket in the Planning Book. Now we will look at the San Diego Factory prior to running the SNP heuristic along with a target stock level modifier.

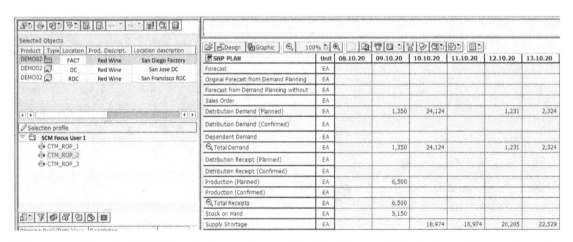

SNP PLAN	Unit	08.10.20	09.10.20	10.10.20	11.10.20	12.10.20	13.10.20
Forecast	EA						
Original Forecast from Demand Planning	EA						
Forecast from Demand Planning without	EA						
Sales Order	EA						
Distribution Demand (Planned)	EA		1,350	24,124		1,231	2,324
Distribution Demand (Confirmed)	EA						
Dependent Demand	EA						
Total Demand	EA		1,350	24,124		1,231	2,324
Distribution Receipt (Planned)	EA						
Distribution Receipt (Confirmed)	EA						
Production (Planned)	EA		6,500				
Production (Confirmed)	EA						
Total Receipts	EA		6,500				
Stock on Hand	EA		5,150				
Supply Shortage	EA			18,974	18,974	20,205	22,529

Before running the SNP heuristic, we have distribution receipts but no planned production. Therefore a supply shortage is shown in the shortage key figure.

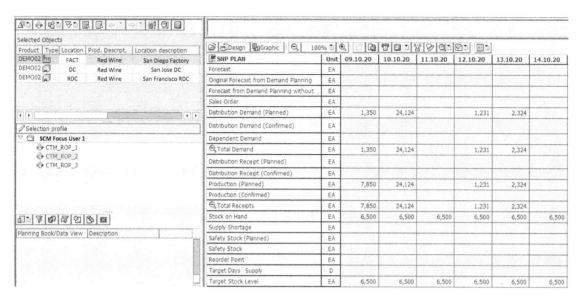

However, after the SNP heuristic is run, we have both planned production orders, as well as a target stock level of 6,500 units maintained by SNP for every planning bucket in the planning horizon (that can be viewed in this screen shot).

Conclusion for Test Two

At this point, we have successfully planned this second test. The final run will again be a CTM pegging run, which has been described in the first test.

Test Three: Run Sequence DC—CTM, RDC—CTM, Factory—Target Days Supply

In this test we will once again change the method that is used at the different echelons. We will also test the SNP heuristic with the target days' supply, a method modifier that we have not used yet. This test will be simpler than the first two because CTM is being used for two of the locations.

The Planning Book Before Step One

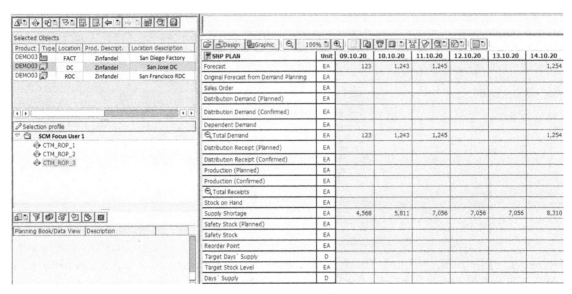

We have demand, but no distribution demand has been created.

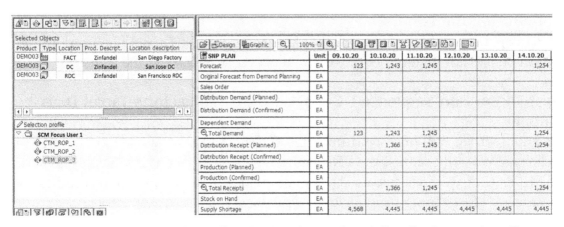

After running CTM, we now have distribution demand and distribution receipts. Because we included both the DC and RDC in the master data selection for CTM, the RDC was processed as well, as can be seen from the screen shot that follows.

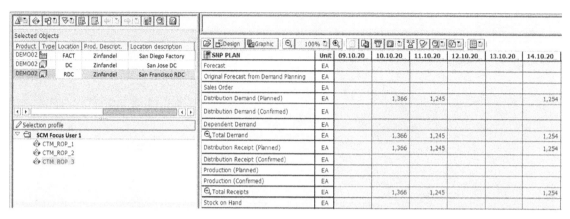

Now that we have successfully planned the DC and RDC, we can move on to the factory.

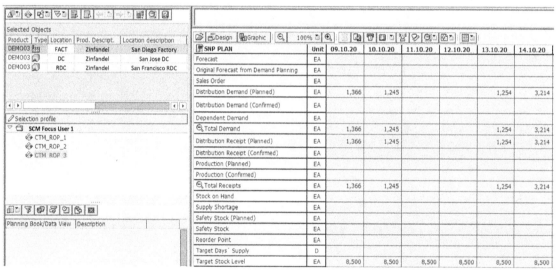

The San Diego Factory Planning Book shows that a target stock level of 6,500 units has been set, and this target value populates all the viewable planning buckets in the Planning Book. After we run the SNP heuristic, we will find that SNP creates planned orders in quantities that will respect this target stock level.

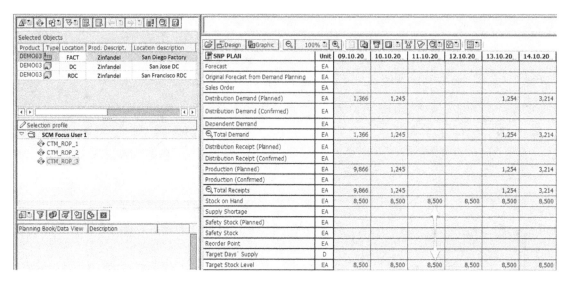

We have successfully planned the three echelons in this test. Next, we need to look at the peggings.

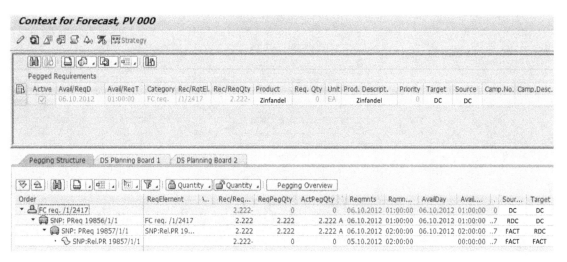

Because the SNP heuristic was used at the factory, there is no pegging beyond the purchase requisition (which again is actually an internal stock transport requisition). In order to rectify this situation, we will run the CTM pegging profile again for the entire supply network for the Zinfandel product.

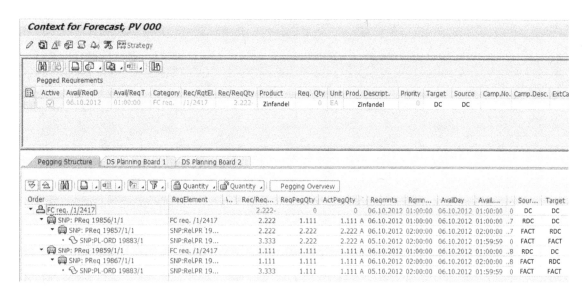

Now we can see the pegging is complete, and the requirement is now pegged to two planned (production) orders.

Conclusion for Test Three

We have successfully planned this third test.

Conclusion

In this chapter, I provided the screen shots for a demonstration of multiple methods and multiple method modifiers. This prototype was designed to test the ability to use different supply planning options together in a single model, and whether the output could make sense. All three tests were effective and I believe that I have demonstrated that multiple methods and method modifiers can be used together. The tests were successful in that the correct values appeared in the correct key figures in the Planning Book. In addition, the pegging screen shots from the product view demonstrated that a logical pegging chain was created from the DC to the finished goods factory. In addition to proving the multi method hypothesis in SNP, this chapter serves as an example of how to document the results of a prototype test.

CHAPTER 6

Coding the Product-Location Database/Spreadsheet

When following a multi method approach, it's important to have a good tool for assigning which method (and method modifier) is to be applied to which product location combination, as well as for keeping track of these assignments. Even though companies have a very large number of product-location combinations, the assignment of methods and method modifiers does not have to be an onerous task. First, a company already has method modifiers set up in their ERP system or external planning system (if they are migrating from another system such as Manugistics). These modifier values can be extracted from the existing system and used. Product-location combinations can be grouped based upon any criteria and have any value applied to them. I am unaware of any approach that is faster or of higher quality than the one I will describe in this chapter.

A major challenge of all application implementations is how to keep track of the settings in the application. This is particularly true of SAP implementations because SAP development takes such a comprehensive approach to developing functionality that every application ends up with a very large number of fields. However, in the vast majority of cases, only a small percentage of the fields are actually used in an implementation. Therefore, one of the most important steps to be performed during the implementation is to determine which fields should have values assigned to them by the business.

In SNP, there are a wide variety of fields in different locations. However, many fields are stored in the product-location master, which is equivalent to the material master in SAP ERP (this would be assigned to a plant to bring in the location dimension). There are hundreds of fields in the product-location master. Most companies only have the values in these fields documented in SAP. However, I believe that to be a mistake. The parameters should be kept in an external database for the following reasons:

1. Product location data cannot be easily compared and contrasted inside of SAP beyond bringing up the product-location master for two combinations in different windows.
2. My preferred way of storing this data is in a spreadsheet, which allows for the filtering of values, the use of Pivot Tables for analysis, and other advanced data capabilities in Excel.
3. Productivity is greatly enhanced when planners have access to the product-location data in an easily accessible form.
4. Visibility, a common problem with product-location data, is enhanced with this approach, reducing the likelihood that this data will become out of date.
5. A product-location spreadsheet can include descriptions and comments in a way that SAP cannot. (Descriptions can be found by hitting F1 from any field. However, descriptions can be placed right in a spreadsheet, and can also be customized—and typically truncated to just the information that is of interest.)
6. This approach applies to setting the overall policies during the initial implementation, and to continued maintenance. Once changes have been made to the spreadsheet, they can be made in SAP APO with the MASSD mass maintenance transaction. MASSD can also be used in conjunction with product-location profiles, which can be efficiently applied to any product-location combination as is described in detail in this article:

    http://www.scmfocus.com/sapplanning/2008/09/13/product-location-profiles-and-mass-maintenance/

Product Location Master Coding Spreadsheet

Field	Product	Location	Planning Method	ATP: Checking Horizon in Days	ATP: Checking Horizon Calendar	Goods Receipt Processing Time
Description			The supply planning method for a product location combination	Defines a time interval (checking date + period) in which a product availability check can be carried out.	The calendar for the checking horizon is used to calculate the end of the checking horizon. It is calculated in work days.	The time between the delivery or the production of a product and its availability as stock.
	White Wine	San Diego Factory	CTM constrained	5	5	2
	White Wine	San Francisco RDC	CTM constrained	5	5	2
	White Wine	San Jose DC	CTM constrained	5	5	2
	White Wine	Encinitas Semi Finished Factory	CTM unconstrained	0	0	1
	White Wine	La Mesa Component Factory	Reorder stock (forward calc basis) from location product master (units)	0	0	1
	White Wine	Napa Semi Finished Factory	Reorder Target Days Supply from location product master (enter days)	0	0	1

This is just a sample of the fields in the product location spreadsheet, and is all that I could fit into this screenshot. There are, of course, many fields on the product-location master. Not all of them are filled in, but it is beneficial to note all of them in the spreadsheet, along with their definitions, so that planners can chose which to enable.

While it can seem intimidating to fill in all the fields of a spreadsheet like this, in fact rarely are the fields filled in one-by-one. It is much more common to group the products for a specific field. Spreadsheets also allow for the applications of if/then formulas, which can auto populate some field values based upon the values of one or more other fields.

Creating this spreadsheet involves many important steps and the spreadsheet has many uses. Considering how valuable it is to document a product-location spreadsheet, the use of this method is a major unrealized opportunity on many projects. I have written extensively on this topic, but this activity continues to be poorly managed on projects and it tends to be confused with or get lost in a loop on master data management (MDM), which I have described in this article:

http://www.scmfocus.com/supplychainmasterdata/2011/05/methodology-for-adjusting-master-data/

How MDM projects have become a major drain on companies is discussed in the following article:

http://www.scmfocus.com/supplychainmasterdata/2010/06/why-software-based-mdm-is-a-consulting-boondoggle/

SAP MDM was a major distraction on SAP projects and never provided value on any of the implementations that I have worked on. Mostly the product has been put on the shelf. SAP has introduced SAP Master Data Governance (MDG), which does not appear to inspire much confidence; as of this writing it only addresses sixty five fields, some of which are relevant for APO and some of which are not. It is unknown whether MDG will make any contribution to APO master data, but given SAP's history in master data applications, I hold little hope that it will. As with relying upon BW reports, there is a high probability that MDG may leave the APO project with a gap.

Steps to Creating the Product-Location Spreadsheet/Database
On the following page I list the steps to creating this product-location spreadsheet, as well as the uses of the product-location spreadsheet.

Creation Steps and Uses of the Product-Location Spreadsheet		
Question	Answer Number	Answers
Usages of the Product-Location Spreadsheet	1	Use a master data mass update tool in order to make the product-location master match the settings in the product-location spreadsheet.
	2	Use the product-location spreadsheet as a reporting device (the spreadsheet can be filtered, sorted, and other Excel data management functions can be used to provide quick evaluation of the settings). Alternatively, the spreadsheet can be imported into a BI application for company-wide reporting.

Once created, the product-location spreadsheet can be reused for many purposes. The following are uses of the product-location spreadsheet.

Creation Steps and Uses of the Product-Location Spreadsheet		
Question	*Answer Number*	*Answers*
Creation Steps of the Product-Location Spreadsheet	1	From evaluating the design, select the fields from the product-location master which may be used by the company.
	2	Review the fields with the business subject matter experts.
	3	Have the business subject matter experts go through and "code" the product-location spreadsheet for every possible product-location combination.

This way of managing settings for applications is quite sustainable, provides a great deal of visibility into the settings, and allows for analysts to easily compare and contrast the parameters. There are some applications, such as BarloWorld's Optimiza application, that build similar functionality right into the user interface, but these types of applications are few and far between. Therefore, in most cases, companies implement software that does not offer this type of functionality. This approach to application settings is quite unusual, as can be seen in the screen shot of Barloworld on the following page:

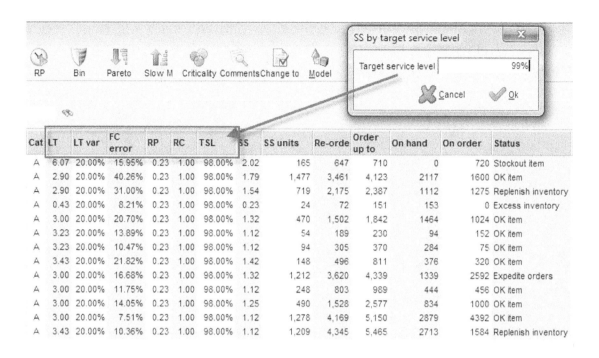

Cat	LT	LT var	FC error	RP	RC	TSL	SS	SS units	Re-orde	Order up to	On hand	On order	Status
A	6.07	20.00%	15.95%	0.23	1.00	98.00%	2.02	165	647	710	0	720	Stockout item
A	2.90	20.00%	40.26%	0.23	1.00	98.00%	1.79	1,477	3,461	4,123	2117	1600	OK item
A	2.90	20.00%	31.00%	0.23	1.00	98.00%	1.54	719	2,175	2,387	1112	1275	Replenish inventory
A	0.43	20.00%	8.21%	0.23	1.00	98.00%	0.23	24	72	151	153	0	Excess inventory
A	3.00	20.00%	20.70%	0.23	1.00	98.00%	1.32	470	1,502	1,842	1464	1024	OK item
A	3.23	20.00%	13.89%	0.23	1.00	98.00%	1.12	54	189	230	94	152	OK item
A	3.23	20.00%	10.47%	0.23	1.00	98.00%	1.12	94	305	370	284	75	OK item
A	3.43	20.00%	21.82%	0.23	1.00	98.00%	1.42	148	496	811	376	320	OK item
A	3.00	20.00%	16.68%	0.23	1.00	98.00%	1.32	1,212	3,620	4,339	1339	2592	Expedite orders
A	3.00	20.00%	11.75%	0.23	1.00	98.00%	1.12	248	803	989	444	456	OK item
A	3.00	20.00%	14.05%	0.23	1.00	98.00%	1.25	490	1,528	2,577	834	1000	OK item
A	3.00	20.00%	7.51%	0.23	1.00	98.00%	1.12	1,278	4,169	5,150	2879	4392	OK item
A	3.43	20.00%	10.36%	0.23	1.00	98.00%	1.12	1,209	4,345	5,465	2713	1584	Replenish inventory

Planners are often told to keep the master data parameters up to date by finding issues and then transferring the values to the master data team for adjustment. Companies generally have no problem understanding the need to have effective planning systems, but often miss the fact that they also need applications to enable these planning parameters to be analyzed and updated, and that they need to provide an effective way for those that have this responsibility to do so.

Barloworld's applications provide the following capabilities:

1. Allows planners to view the overall supply network.
2. Notifies planners about what to focus their attention on.
3. Allows the planners to manipulate supply planning parameters.
4. Provides planners with an understanding of the relationship between different supply planning elements.

A number of Barloworld's screens are examples of what I am referring to when I describe supply chain visibility. The following view highlights the obvious areas to be addressed by the planner. The categories F, M, and N on the next page are carrying far too much inventory according to what the Barloworld model recommends. Armed with this information, the planner can then go into the necessary details to determine why this is the case and take corrective action.

Category		Actual		Model	
Cat ▲	Count	Value	Cover	Value	Cover
A	205	$1,805,399.92	1.34	$954,113.93	0.71
B	674	$1,609,338.85	1.38	$1,099,283.35	0.98
C	762	$701,378.75	1.80	$324,462.58	0.81
D	811	$516,177.63	2.65	$234,015.15	1.15
E	1,236	$290,272.74	2.13	$220,842.01	1.51
F	11,741	$2,194,308.21	37.61	$136,801.50	2.00
M	2,859	$639,104.04	4.50	$278,735.34	1.12
N	1,148	$136,600.67	8.86	$11,860.99	0.54
X	0	$0.00	0.00	$0.00	0.00
Total	19,436	$7,892,580.81	2.29	$3,260,114.85	0.91

The quality of the application's interface is frequently overlooked in all methods of supply planning. Some of the most popular supply planning applications are, in fact, quite poor at providing supply chain visibility and require extensive external reports to be created in order to compensate for the weakness of the interface (which as has been discussed, ends up being a placebo if the company chooses a poor reporting application such as SAP BW).

http://www.scmfocus.com/enterprisesoftwarepolicy/2011/12/11/could-dp-or-the-bw-survive-as-independent-products-from-sap/

http://www.scmfocus.com/enterprisesoftwarepolicy/2011/11/29/how-efficient-is-the-market-for-enterprise-software/

Visibility in Supply Planning Systems

The important aspects of visibility in supply planning software are outlined below:

1. The planner should be able to see things such as valid location-to-location combinations (some locations only ship to certain locations) or valid product-to-location combinations (which products are stocked at which locations) in the supply network. SNP can do this—in a way, with an elementary filter, which restricts the locations shown based upon products or vice versa. One can also leverage the Supply Chain Engineer transaction, which I discuss below, but I have never been able to match an external spreadsheet in terms of flexibility, speed or usability in any supply planning application much less SNP. Therefore, yet another application of this spreadsheet once completed, is as a reference document.

2. The system should display the status of a product location, such as the stock transfers, purchase orders, stock and important measures.

3. The application should display the parameters that are assigned to each product-location combination. They include values such as lead times and safety stock, which traditionally companies have a great deal of difficulty both analyzing and maintaining.

Conclusion

The documentation of product-location master data through the use of an external spreadsheet is a proven, yet underutilized, technique of determining which methods, method modifiers and other master data parameters are applied to product-location combinations. The spreadsheet delivers value, all the way from its initial development to its use as a reference document to help multiple individuals make sense of how the supply planning system is set up.

The spreadsheet approach applies to demand planning, production planning, etc. However, as this book focuses only on supply planning, I have limited the discussion to the context of the subject matter of this book. The product-location spreadsheet is even more important when applying the multi-method approach outlined in this book, as it can easily be used to store and retrieve the method that is being used to plan a product-location combination. (Chapter 5: "Prototyping the Multi Method Supply Planning Model" will describe how to use an approach to signify the method with one of the standard custom fields on the product location master in APO. Beyond identification, this field can also be used to set up dynamic selections to switch any product location between any supply planning method by the simple act of changing this field.) Using a spreadsheet to store parameters meets all of the requirements that I have laid out in this chapter for how companies should manage this data.

CHAPTER 7

Planning Beyond a Single Supply Planning Method Per Echelon

The three tests that were performed in Chapter 5: "Prototyping the Multi Method Supply Planning Model" showed that different supply planning methods could be applied per echelon. However, it would be the rare implementation that would want to use a single method per echelon for all product locations. Some echelons may use one method universally; however, multiple methods would be applied in at least some of the echelons. Companies that commit to a multi method approach to supply planning will want the ability to set any method for any product location. See the following matrix for what this would look like:

Products

Location	White Wine	Red Wine	Zinfandel	Run Sequence
San Jose DC	CTM	CTM	Target Days' Supply	1. CTM for White Wine & Red Wine 2. Heuristic for Zinfandel
San Francisco RDC	CTM	Target Stocking Level	CTM	3. CTM for White Wine & Zinfandel 4. Heuristic for Red Wine
San Diego Factory (Bottling)	Target Days' Supply	CTM	CTM	5. CTM for White Wine 6. Heuristic for Zinfandel
BOM	Wine, Cork, Bottle Label	Wine, Cork, Bottle Label	Wine, Cork, Bottle Label	
Napa Winery	Unmodified Heuristic	Reorder Point w/ forecast	Reorder Point w/o forecast	7. Heuristic for All
San Diego Winery	Unmodified Heuristic	Unmodified Heuristic	Unmodified Heuristic	8. Heuristic for All

In this example, we have changed the methods not only up to the finished goods factory, but have also added the bill of material and the components—which are brought in from wineries (wine), as well as procured (cork, bottle, label). The same principle applies below the finished goods factory as above it.

As you see, the approach is to plan echelon by echelon. That is, the network must be processed top down, so that distribution demands and distribution receipts will cascade through the network.

In the three tests demonstrated in Chapter 7: "Prototyping the Multi Method Supply Planning Model," a single method was run per echelon, so there was no question of sequence within that echelon. With multiple methods per echelon, the question of method sequence within the echelon is an issue. However, because of the way material flows through a supply network, the supply planning method sequence does not need to be accounted for in the design because the initial supply plan, as well as the deployment plan, work through a controlled system of "parent" and "child" locations (although here we focus on the initial supply plan; for a full explanation of the differences between the initial supply plan and the deployment plan see my book, *Supply Planning with MRP, DRP and APS Software*).

However, redeployment works completely differently in terms of which locations can send stock to which other locations. During the specialized redeployment run, there is interaction between all the locations—horizontal and vertical—in the supply network, although this is a separate run with its own logic. In fact, redeployment does not exist in SNP—not in standard functionality and not by making special adjustments to the standard functionality. Most companies that implement APO and require redeployment functionality create a custom report or an external custom program, or purchase a best of breed application that has this functionality. This topic is discussed in more detail in the article below:

http://www.scmfocus.com/inventoryoptimizationmultiechelon/2011/10/redeployment/

However, in SNP, if redeployment stock transport orders are created outside of APO, transportation lanes must exist between the locations in APO in order for the STOs sent to SNP to be processed. This issue, and the resolution to the issue, is discussed on the next page.

Horizontal versus Vertical Location-to-Location Interaction

In the vast majority of cases, the locations at the same echelon level (i.e., all DCs, all RDCs, all factories) do not interact with one another. The interaction is vertical in the supply network (between DCs and RDCs, and RDCs to factories, etc.) and not horizontal. Therefore, as long as each parent echelon is processed for a product location before the child location, the distribution demand can be effectively passed between locations without issue. While providing the ability to use a variety of supply planning methods per product location in the supply network may sound challenging, it isn't much more challenging than what has already been demonstrated. It will work, as long as the rule of echelon processing sequence is adhered to. Once the profiles and variants are set up for each (which

I very much recommend organizing in a spreadsheet before setting up in SAP), the overall supply plan will be coherent.

Effectively Combining Other Methods Not Explained in the Prototype

The previous section showed that multiple heuristic-based methods can be used along with CTM. But what about other methods, such as the cost optimizer, inventory optimization and multi echelon planning? Well, the cost optimizer, which is the final method available within SNP, can also be used along with any of the methods shown above. Prior to the cost optimizer being run, distribution demand must be created in the product location to be planned by the cost optimizer. As long as that rule is followed, there should be no problem planning any product-location combination with the cost optimizer. Combining SNP with the methods not available in SNP, such as inventory optimization and multi echelon planning, is covered in Chapter 10: "Combining SNP with Inventory Optimization and Multi Echelon Planning."

Conclusion

The prototype tests that were performed in Chapter 5: "Prototyping the Multi Method Supply Planning Model" used one method per echelon in the supply network. In real life, different methods and method modifiers will be run for at least some of the echelons. This requirement can be easily met by always processing the supply network from "top to bottom" and in sequence, such that the distribution centers are processed first, then the regional distribution centers, and then the finished goods factory and so on. This rule of thumb works well because the interaction between locations is vertical and not horizontal during the initial supply plan and during the deployment (although not the redeployment planning run). Processing the supply network echelon by echelon enforces the vertical flow through the supply network.

CHAPTER 8

Creating a Dynamic Master Data Selection for Automatic Product Location Switching Between Methods

One of the issues that surfaces with the use of multiple methods is that long-term maintenance is higher than with a single method approach. It is certainly simple to use a single method for the entire supply network. In fact, all of the methods in SNP can be run without any product-location specification, and for all products and all locations. However, after a number of years working on supply planning projects, I think it is the rare instance where this would meet all of the business requirements.

Under the multi method approach, product-location combinations must be switched between different methods. As time passes, the underlying demand characteristics of product-location combinations change, which naturally migrates them to a different way of being planned. Secondly, new products must be added to SNP which were not previously part of the product-location database. These activities can be automated by using something called a dynamic master data selection or a "dynamic selection" for short. A dynamic selection is different from a static master data selection and a different way of running any of the supply planning methods.

Understanding the Static Master Data Selection

In most cases, the different supply planning methods are run off of static selections of master data (i.e., product-location combinations). A static selection hard codes a particular combination or products and locations into a variant or profile. Any number of variants or profiles can be created, but each variant or profile is unchanging. For example, a static selection would look like the following:

Supply Network Planning: Planning Run

⊕ ⬓ Display Logs

Data Source

Planning Book	9ASNP94
Data View	SNP94(1)
Global SNP Settings Profile	SAP
Paral. Proc. Profile	

◉ Entire Planning Horizon
○ Planning Horizon in Days | 0

Object Selection

○ Selection Profile

    Selection Profile | | 👓

◉ Manual Selection

Planning Version	000		
Product Number	Red Wine	to	➡
Location	San Jose DC	to	➡
Low-Level Code		to	➡

Scope of Planning

◉ Network (Heuristic)
○ Location (Heuristic)
☑ Take into account found components in planning run
☑ Add products from supersession chains
☐ Net Change Planning

Source Determination	All Levels ▼
Temporary Low-Level Codes	Do not use temporary low-level codes ▼

Above, you can see that the product, Red Wine, for the San Jose DC is hard coded into this particular SNP heuristic variant.

An unlimited number of profiles can be created that are assigned to different static master data sets, so it might seem that there is great flexibility built into this design, yet it does not allow for adjusting master data in a flexible manner. However, the dynamic selection, which is much less frequently used, provides the ability for each method profile or variant to remain untouched, but for product-location combinations to be dynamically assigned to them by changing a field on the product-location master. While the dynamic selection only exists inside of CTM—and not the SNP heuristic or the SNP cost optimizer—there are ways of forcing the SNP heuristic and SNP cost optimizer to work in a dynamic way, as I will demonstrate. Since the dynamic selection is only in CTM, we will begin the demonstration there.

The CTM Dynamic Master Data Selection

With the CTM screen shot on the following page you can see that the dynamic selection can be based upon either a product-location combination (therefore, product-location combinations that are no longer valid would not be processed by CTM) or more powerfully, by pointing to a field on the product-location master. Five custom fields are available on the product-location master to use by the implementation. Any one of these fields can represent the categories of product locations that are to be planned in a different way (assigned to a type of planning method profile). Therefore, whenever a product location must be assigned to a new method, all that is required is for the adjustment to be made on this field in the product-location master.

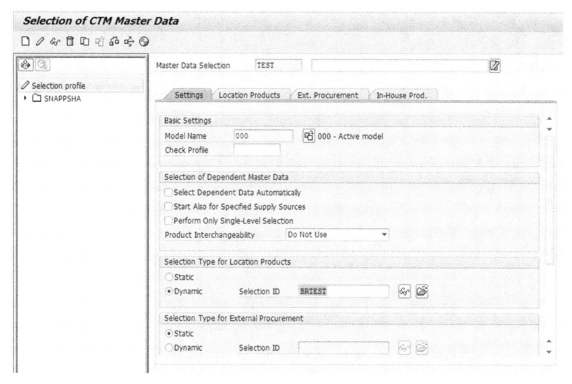

Here we can see that dynamic selection is an option within the master data selection for CTM. The first step to using the dynamic selection is to create a dynamic master data selection.

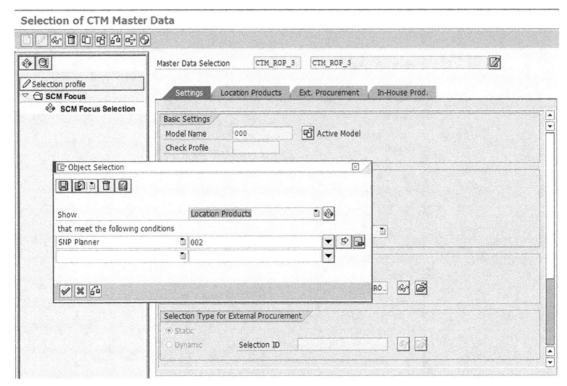

Here I am creating a dynamic selection. In CTM, this is accomplished from within the master data selection screen. Once inside, I select the "clover" or "flower" button and add the selection that I want to apply. I could use any number of fields to create the relationship between the field on the product-location master and the dynamic selection. In this case, I am using the SNP Planner.

Selection of CTM Master Data

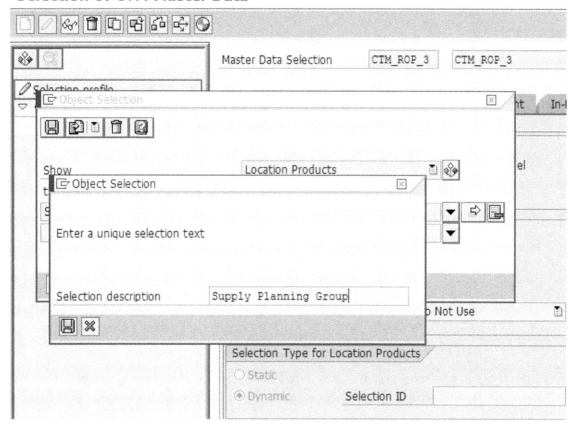

Here I am naming the dynamic selection "Supply Planning Group."

Selection of CTM Master Data

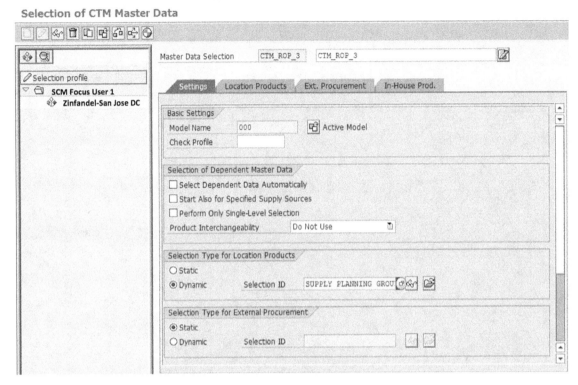

Here the dynamic selection that was created is applied to the dynamic selection in the SNP master data selection. This master data selection is then applied to the CTM Profile.

It would certainly be nice if the SNP heuristic and the SNP cost optimizer also had a dynamic selection option for its master data. If it did, it would be exceedingly easy to switch among all the methods in SNP. Now I will cover how to get the SNP heuristic and cost optimizer to behave essentially the same way.

Pseudo Dynamic Selection with the SNP Heuristic and the SNP Cost Optimizer

Both the SNP heuristic and the SNP cost optimizer assign the master data selection (product-location combinations) to an SNP heuristic or SNP cost optimizer run the same way, through either the Manual Selection or by assigning the variant or profile to a pre-created Selection Profile. This is shown in the following screen shot.

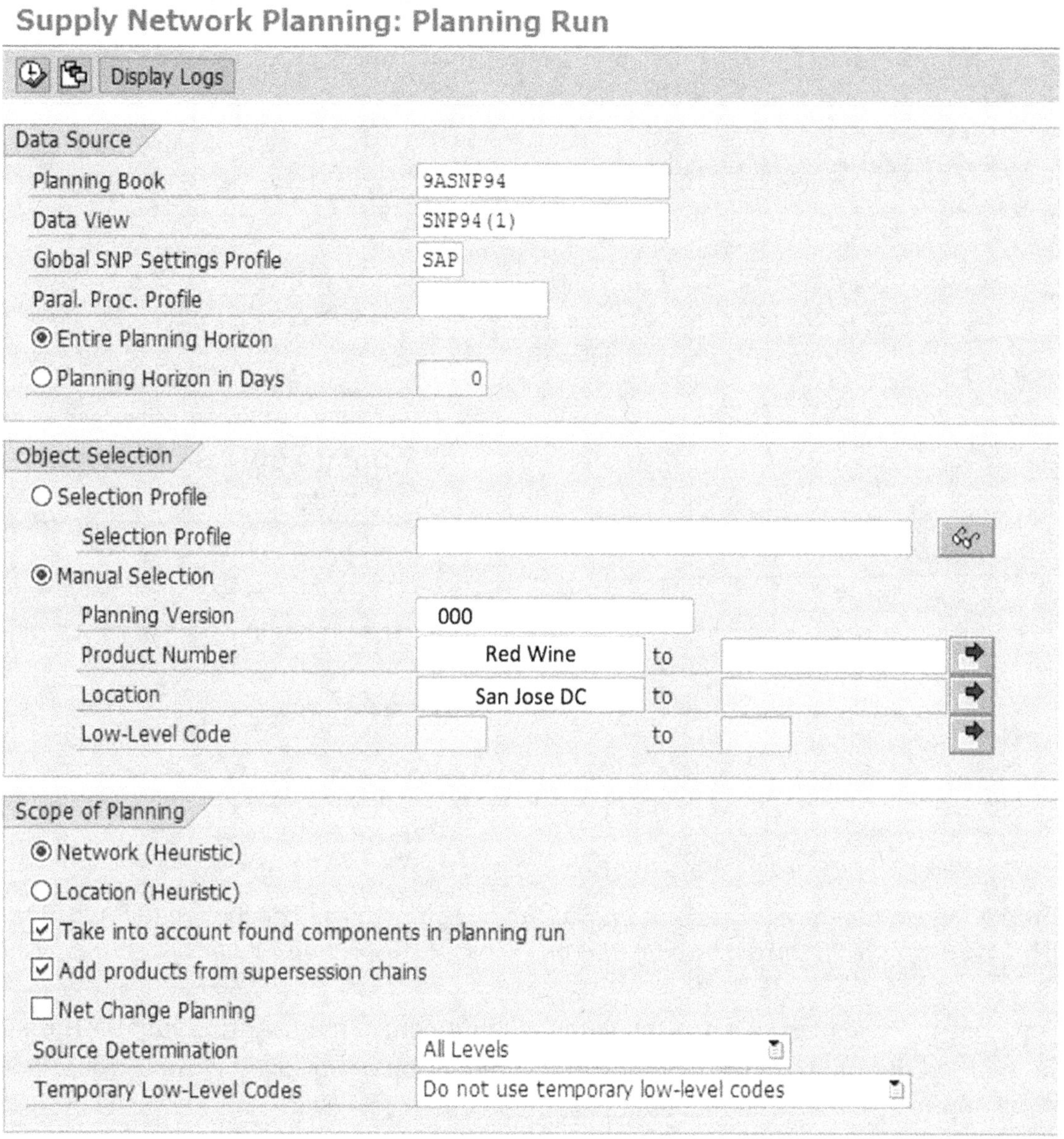

Supply Network Planning: Planning Run

⊕ 🔁 Display Logs

Data Source

Planning Book	9ASNP94
Data View	SNP94(1)
Global SNP Settings Profile	SAP
Paral. Proc. Profile	

- ◉ Entire Planning Horizon
- ○ Planning Horizon in Days   0

Object Selection

- ○ Selection Profile
  - Selection Profile   [   ]   🔍
- ◉ Manual Selection
  - Planning Version   000

Product Number	Red Wine	to		➡
Location	San Jose DC	to		➡
Low-Level Code		to		➡

Scope of Planning

- ◉ Network (Heuristic)
- ○ Location (Heuristic)
- ☑ Take into account found components in planning run
- ☑ Add products from supersession chains
- ☐ Net Change Planning

Source Determination	All Levels
Temporary Low-Level Codes	Do not use temporary low-level codes

This is the screen that is used to run the SNP heuristic. When, as I have shown above, data is entered into this screen and saved, a variant is created.

The SNP cost optimizer is different in that there is one screen/transaction (with multiple tabs) to set up the optimizer profile, and one screen/transaction to run the optimizer.

However, the two methods are the same when it comes to assigning master data to the method during the run. If the Manual Selection is not used (which would be a static approach), then the Selection Profile is used. The Selection Profile is created in the Planning Book. When selecting a product-location combination, there are many alternatives that can be entered. This is what the Selection Profile is using to select the specific product locations that will be processed by the planning run.

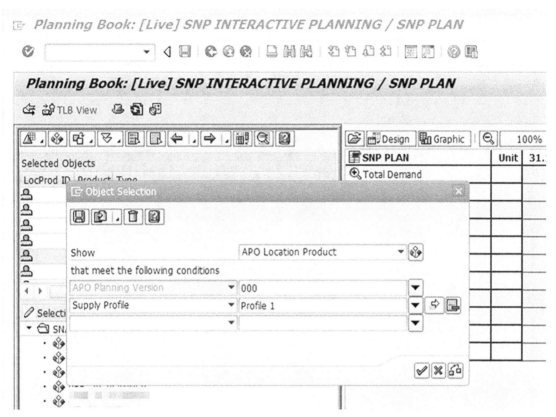

A new Selection Profile is created by clicking the Selection Window button (which is the three-pronged flower button second from the far right). In the Selection Profile I am creating above, I have selected the Supply Profile. The Supply Profile is one of the five profiles that are used to assign master data parameters to groups of product-location combinations. If this option is used, then the same method can be applied to the same product locations, which are categorized by the Supply Profile, or by any of the five different profiles that are available. The implementation can choose to use an active profile or one that is not being used, so that the only purpose of the profile becomes to assign product-location combinations to different methods.

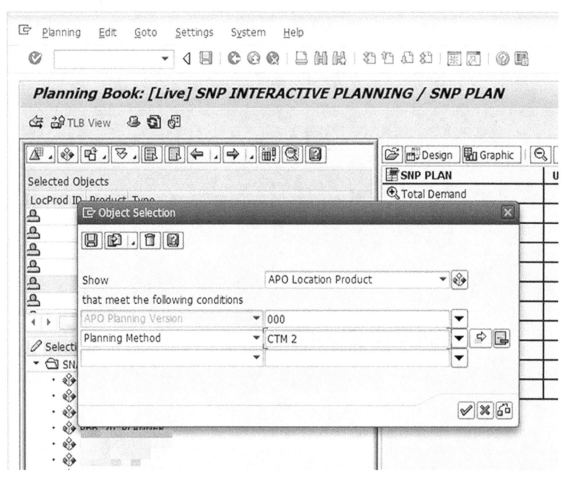

Another option is to select a custom field. There are five custom fields on the product-location master, and they can be named any name and assigned to the Selection Profile. Having a custom field named "Planning Method," and using it to control the Selection Profile would be very good for visibility. It would also allow any person looking through the product-location master to know which product locations are assigned to which planning methods.

What this demonstrates is that all three methods in SNP can be controlled with a "dynamic selection." With CTM, the dynamic selection is part of the standard functionality, but with both the SNP cost optimizer as well as the SNP heuristic a dynamic selection can be emulated with some creative usage of the Selection

Profile, and in some cases the adoption of one of the five open custom fields on the product-location master. This means that any product-location combination in the database can be assigned between the different methods by simply updating what would be possibly one (all methods could use the custom field) or at most two fields on the product-location master.

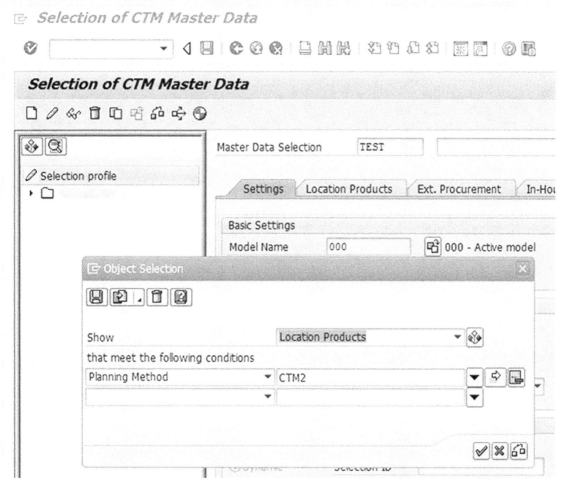

Here, back in the CTM master data selection screen, we can also key the CTM profile to process all product-location combinations that have the coding "CTM2" in the Planning Method (which is a renamed custom field).

Conclusion

Using dynamic master data selection for all the methods in SNP is an important foundational configuration approach for creating a lower-maintenance design for a multi method supply planning approach. Setting up the configuration includes the following steps:

1. Set up the dynamic selection in CTM.
2. Determine which custom field to leverage for keying the Selection Profiles for the SNP heuristic variant and the SNP cost optimizer profile.
3. Create Selection Profiles for the SNP heuristic and the SNP cost optimizer.
4. Point to the chosen field (either custom or standard) in the Selection Profiles.

CHAPTER 9

Overcoming the Human and Information Challenges of the Multi Method Approach

Information Challenges

As I noted in Chapter 1: "Introduction," there is a shortage of information published on the use of mixed supply planning methods. As an implementation consultant, I learned about mixing methods through trial and error in order to meet business requirements. You may ask why so little is written on the topic; let us take a look at some of the usual suspects who might be expected to cover mixed supply planning methods.

1. *Academics:* This topic would not be considered "original research" as none of the methods employed is original, even though the combination of the methods is in fact original. As such, any academic that attempted to publish on such a topic would probably run into a problem getting the paper published.

2. *Companies that Implement Enterprise Supply Planning Software:* Software implementation consulting companies don't really do research. While many of the major consulting companies have "research" departments, none are respected because they are all simply extensions of the sales department. They provide no coverage on the topic of multiple supply planning methods, and

it's a challenge for any of them to produce accurate information, much less "research" as pointed out in the following article:

http://www.scmfocus.com/inventoryoptimizationmultiechelon/2010/10/ booz-allen-hamilton-misrepresents-inventory-optimization-in-white-papers/

3. *Analysts:* To perform research in this area, one either has to test software in a lab environment or perform the testing on actual implementations. The analyst firms don't actually get their hands on software and also do not produce research of this type.

4. *Software Vendors in Supply Planning:* The thought leaders for practical implementation research are the software vendors. However, this type of research is not an area of focus for them. In fact, if a software vendor has a product that uses one particular method, they certainly are not going to publish research on how competing methods perform. For instance, SAP created a partnership with an inventory optimization and multi echelon planning (MEIO) vendor called SmartOps, not because of some research conclusion that MEIO blended well with older methods of supply planning, but because SAP needed a solution for customers who were asking about MEIO functionality. By partnering with SmartOps, they were able to use their monopoly power in APO to resell a new technology. In other words, sales are primary and research is secondary, at least in the enterprise software market. When there are sales involved, a vendor's objectivity steeply declines, with every vendor declaring that their particular method—or their customization of the method—is the best on the market.

In searches on the Internet and through books on Amazon and Google Books, etc., the only substantial research I was able to find on mixed methods was in articles at SCM Focus.com. (Of course, I hope this book is able to help change this state of affairs.) In fact, SAP's own documentation on SNP presents the alternatives in very binary terms as the following quote demonstrates:

> *Most customers then run either the SNP Optimizer or the SNP*
> *Heuristic, depending on the size of the problem and whether they can*
> *meet their needs with the infinite planning considered by the Heuristic.*
> — Best Practice: Manage Supply Network Planning & CTM in APO, SAP

As a result of the lack of research into mixed methods, consultants and other practitioners have very little to read on this topic. They don't hear about mixed methods, so quite often they seem to assume that it is not a normal practice.

Human Challenges to Implementing the Mixed Method Approach

I believe there is a strong tendency for implementation consultants in general to offer a limited menu of method alternatives to their clients. In some ways this is strange or at least inconsistent; my observation is that the average consultant tends to propose overly complex alternatives to their clients, due in part to what I call "résumé building." While a very complex and unsustainable functionality may not do anything for the business (or even be counterproductive), the consultant can still place the skill and experience gained through the project on his or her résumé. The market for consultants in SAP is competitive, and everyone is looking for an edge. Clients want diverse experience in a variety of functionalities within a particular module. SAP itself promotes nonfunctional "gingerbread house" implementations by rushing out functionality before it is ready and allowing their customers to perform their bug identification and testing for them. Many consultants may say that all enterprise vendors work this way, but I would have to disagree. Of all the vendors I work with, SAP is the most brazen about releasing both unfinished new products and unfinished new functionality to existing products.

Some consultants simply work from the perspective of "whatever worked best for them on their last project." In fact, the more technically savvy consultants seem to have less neural plasticity when it comes to interpreting and applying business requirements to their configuration, even though this is a skill that clients—who often simply produce a laundry list of desired configuration experience—would like to have in a consultant but don't seem to get. Experience is not enough; the consultant must have the plasticity to adjust to new requirements.

Also, in APO, most consultants are not well-versed in the research behind the various methods. Many of the technical consultants, who are efficient APO jockeys, are passing themselves off as inventory and supply planning business specialists when in fact, they are not. These consultants have a tendency to think that the business is misguided in using "less sophisticated" methods. I have often heard the criticism that if only the company would improve its forecast, then mixed methods would not be necessary (because more products would be forecastable). The "if we just improved the forecast error" argument is a Swiss Army Knife: it can be brought out in many different situations but does not provide any insight or value to the decision at hand. This argument is also used against implementing a redeployment run in order to reposition stock to where it can be consumed, but the argument never makes any sense.

Why the Continual Promise of Forecast Accuracy is Not a Way Out of Finding Supply Planning Solutions

The following explains why the promise of forecast accuracy is not a way of avoiding solutions for supply planning:

1. *Forecast Accuracy Over Time:* Extensive exposure to many companies leads me to the conclusion that, after decades of implementing forecasting software, forecasting accuracy has not improved very much. We don't know the exact details because there is no research in this area beyond self-reported surveys.

2. *Manual or System Forecast Error?* By and large, companies have no idea what percentage of their forecast error is related to manual overrides versus the system-generated forecast.

    (http://www.scmfocus.com/demandplanning/2012/02/how-much-can-your-forecasting-accuracy-be-improved/)

3. *The Rise of Product Proliferation:* Product proliferation has made it more difficult to attain good forecast accuracy. Very few companies have marketing departments that actually develop a strategy that is friendly to the supply chain. One of the few that does is showcased in the following article:

    http://www.scmfocus.com/demandplanning/2012/03/how-trader-joes-reduces-lumpy-demand/

4. *Poor Software Selections:* Companies continue to select inappropriate forecasting software for their needs. See this link for more details:

    http://www.scmfocus.com/demandplanning/2010/09/why-companies-are-selecting-the-wrong-supply-chain-demand-planning-systems/

5. *Bad Advice on Forecasting Software:* Most of the major consulting companies are aligned with some of the worst forecasting products, because the worst forecasting products tend to come from the largest vendors. (Several exceptions are Manugistics, SAS, and possibly Oracle with Demantra, but the longer Oracle owns Demantra—an acquisition—the more it will likely fall behind.) For the most part, the large consulting companies enjoy their financial interests above their clients. Doing so means great personal and corporate financial success, and is how one becomes a highly respected partner at these companies.

   (http//www.scmfocus.com/consulting/why-big-consulting-firms-cannot-do-software-selection/)

6. *Attribute-Based Forecasting:* This has been one of the most important improvements to forecasting in the past decade. However, most companies don't understand the concept and use software that has weak or incomplete attribute-based functionality. Lengthy and unnecessary meetings take place on the topics of aggregation/disaggregation or characteristic value combinations, all because companies are using dated forecasting software. In fact, even at the time of publication, the term "attribute" is rarely used or searched for on the Internet.

   (http://www.scmfocus.com/demandplanning/2012/02/why-isnt-attribute-based-forecasting-a-more-popular-term/)

7. *The Desire to Falsify Forecast Accuracy Measurement:* Most companies are bad at forecasting and many VPs and directors of forecasting have little knowledge about forecasting. Fortunately, vendors have decided to offer them a way to cover up their high forecast error. This category of software is called "demand sensing" and its only real purpose is to assist companies in falsifying their forecast accuracy. Of course, the worse a company is at forecasting, the more attractive demand-sensing software is to them. This falls under the catchphrase "if you can't make it, fake it."

   (http://www.scmfocus.com/demandplanning/2012/01/demand-shaping-and-demand-sensing/)

Therefore, most companies are not even following the most elementary principles of forecasting, so the expectations of forecast accuracy improvement should be greatly tempered. Forecasting is such a problem that I have proposed outsourcing it to companies that specialize in forecasting.

http://www.scmfocus.com/demandplanning/2012/03/outsourced-forecasting/

Of course, I am biased as SCM Focus offers such a service. Why would outsourcing work in forecasting while it has been such a disaster in IT support? Read the article above to find out.

An extensive explanation of the inability of companies to take advantage of forecasting technologies is chronicled in my book, *Supply Chain Forecasting Software*.

Why Advanced Planning Consultants Often Question a Multi Method Approach

Most APO consultants are technical resources, but since they are able to configure APO, they are under the illusion that they have a deep understanding of the business and operations research side of supply planning.

However, when consultants in APO who are primarily technical want to get into the discussion of whether reorder points or target days' supply or another method should be used, they quickly find themselves out of their depth. In most cases the typical APO consultant will not be up to date on why different methods should be used, and SAP itself is not populated by subject matter experts in inventory management, forecasting, etc. Therefore, what often occurs is a consultant with an undergraduate degree in engineering or computer science (often an MBA, but without any supply chain concentration), who has never worked in planning, questions the planning approaches of people with far more experience.

I have never taken this approach. As I stated in Chapter 2: "The Different Supply Planning Methods Available within SAP SNP," the actual role of the software implementation consultant is to translate the business requirements into the configuration, not to choose the methods by which the business will perform planning. It's natural that everyone would want to enlarge his or her role, when this occurs projects work a lot less smoothly. This problem is not restricted to SAP consultants. I wrote the following article for a business lead who was new to software implementations and who thought that her role was to decide for the business what the design should be, rather than walking them through the process and allowing them to decide.

http://www.scmfocus.com/sapprojectmanagement/2010/06/the-role-of-the-business-lead/

Sometimes consultants simply don't know or have never had their role explained to them. However, in most cases where SAP implementation consultants overstep their boundaries, it's often because they are attempting to be more in control of the settings by undermining the input from the business. This gets into the topic of "best practices," an approach proposed primarily as a sales strategy by SAP and the major consulting companies. Sometimes the partners in large consulting companies who, as they tend to be egomaniacs, continually encourage their consultants to "take control of the implementation" reinforce this behavior. The following article describes this approach at one of the major APO implementing consulting companies:

http://www.scmfocus.com/sapprojectmanagement/2011/07/the-ibm-systems-implementation-approach/

However, I would remind these consultants, and the partners that hold their leashes, that they eventually leave the company while the business has to live with the settings for a long time.

Legitimate Concerns Regarding the Multi Method Approach

However, even very flexible and well-meaning supply planning software implementation resources can have trouble with the concept of the multi-method approach in terms of how to pull it off from a technical perspective. For instance, I worked with one SNP resource that was simply concerned whether multiple methods would work due to their complexity. Many of the concerns he brought up were quite valid and are helpful for others to read. I have paraphrased his statement for less technical readers:

"There is one more thing we should bear in mind in connection with this topic: the SNP Heuristic works with a low-level code determination (for determining the sequence of product-location processing). Unfortunately, it is unable to handle loops in the network. For example, if you have bi-directional transportation lanes for redeployment purposes—that is, two separate transportation lanes for the same products going in opposite directions—the heuristic will fail. CTM, however, is completely independent from low-level code (it ranks orders instead of planning objects). According to our test, CTM is happy to plan supply chains containing loops. So if we want to have bi-directional (e.g., cross-DC) transportation lanes in the network, then we will not be able to use the heuristic at all."

Below is my response to him:

"That is an interesting observation. So let's get into the low-level code determination.

They are the processing sequence of the method. In fact, I proposed that the term 'low-level code' is completely nondescriptive, and they could better be referred to as the 'location product run sequence.' In modeling speak, they are the location and product decomposition logic or queue.

In order to evaluate how the SNP heuristic and the low-level codes work with a multi method approach, let's keep it to two products in a network with four locations: 1,2,3,4.

So the low-level code can tell the SNP heuristic to run in the sequence

1. *A1, A2, B1, B2, A3, B3, A4, B4 or*
2. *A4, B4, A3, B3, A2, B2, ,A1, B1*

...or any other combination. More on the low-level code can be read at the link below:

http://www.scmfocus.com/sapplanning/2011/02/04/level-of-bom-planning-in-the-snp-heuristic-and-low-level-codes/

However, this is only the for the initial supply plan. The redeployment is completely separate. So we can set up any combination of CTM and the SNP heuristic, and the initial supply plan should run fine. A new run (and let's just imagine for a minute that some type of CTM run was created for redeployment) should not impact the settings for the initial supply plan. Furthermore, I have never seen SNP used for redeployment anywhere. I have spent a lot of time on redeployment, including studying the logic of redeployment at the vendors that are the best at it: service parts planning vendors. I have several PDF manuals on my laptop from these vendors with the logic and parameters, and this logic shows the correct way to set up a deployment. No method makes any sense for redeployment in SNP. That is sort of the theoretical outer boundary of the topic. However, if we return to the practical project context, redeployment can be managed by a report, so we would not need bi-directional lanes. Therefore, in my view, it's not an issue.

I see the benefits of the multi method approach to be quite large. However, there are costs, but the costs I would be more concerned about are socializing the solution (which is not particularly challenging, but I keep running into poorly socialized solutions so I thought I would bring it up), and the extra complexity in the configuration and maintenance. I think we have mostly addressed the maintenance issue with the dynamic selection profile, which is really a great thing. I think we also have substantially lessened the complexity by planning all product locations in APO, rather than splitting them between APO and ERP.

Obviously, you will have to decide the best approach for the future. I can say that the business case for the mixed method approach is very clear. It's not as easy to implement as a single method approach, but I think it's the right solution."

His response is below:

"In order to reflect an externally determined or manually created redeployment, redeployment stock transport orders are necessary between DCs. This means transportation lanes must be set up in SNP in order for stock transport orders to come over from SAP ERP to SAP APO/ SCM. This is true if STOs are created in SAP ERP. In fact, the CIF— which moves STOs from SAP ERP to SAP APO/SCM—will not be able to bring STOs over to SAP APO/SCM that are created in ECC.

Once redeployment transportation lanes are set up in APO, we can only run the SNP heuristic for location-product combinations that are used by those transportation lanes by temporarily disabling the products on transportation lanes during the SNP heuristic run. This is accomplished by setting the transportation lanes to a blocked status. However, as redeployment logic means that any location can send stock to any location, quite a few redeployment lanes must be set up and then switched on and switched off. It would be most desirable to automate this process. This might be possible in the process chain, which would trigger the MASSD transaction which is a Mass Update."

My response to him is as follows:

"Yes, you are, of course, right. But, I think the risk, or the size of the issue and maintenance depends upon frequency. Essentially what we would be doing is setting up two different supply networks: one for the initial supply plan and deployment and one for redeployment.

Companies that run redeployment almost always do so intermittently. That is, it is not a weekly thread. They may run the redeployment quarterly, or twice per quarter. There can also be things called special deployment runs that are in response to a specific event. One example I have seen is a run to rebalance stock that was brought into locations due to some type of discount. So a company gets a 20 percent reduction if they buy some product in bulk, but they have to bring all of it to one location to qualify for the discount. As insufficient demand exists to consume that stock at the arrival location, the stock must be redeployed.

But if we assume a redeployment run every four to six weeks, the effort of flipping the blocked indicator off on the redeployment transportation lanes for STOs to flow over to SNP and then flipping them back with MASSD does not seem like a lot of work to me. But as I have never set up this exact design, I can't say for sure if we would run into problems. So I suppose it would be yet another test item."

Interestingly, after I wrote this I learned that this particular company wanted to run redeployment once per week, one of the highest frequencies I had ever heard of. For more on redeployment, see this link:

http://www.scmfocus.com/inventoryoptimizationmultiechelon/2011/10/redeployment/

This frequency meant that the automatic switching on and off of transportation lanes was something that would have to be scheduled weekly.

Conclusion

Most of this book has focused on the business and technical aspects of setting up a multi method supply planning model. However, the human component is just as important.

One challenge faced by companies wishing to employ a multi method approach outlined in this book is the fact that very little is published on the topic, meaning that most SNP implementers are not familiar with this approach. SAP explains SNP as being used in a very binary fashion, using one of the three methods exclusively for the implementation.

Because many SNP consultants are unfamiliar with the multi method approach, I think the majority of them would resist using it. Most have not done the testing that I have done, which shows that the approach can be made to work and can be made sustainable, especially when things such as dynamic master data selections are employed.

CHAPTER 10

Combining SNP with Inventory Optimization and Multi Echelon Planning

The way that inventory optimization and multi echelon planning (MEIO) are integrated with all the other supply planning methods is quite different from what has been described thus far. (For a detailed explanation of MEIO see my book, *Inventory Optimization and Multi Echelon Planning Software.*) For one thing, the MEIO method of supply planning does not exist within SNP, making it unfeasible to turn on some product locations for MEIO and some locations for CTM, the SNP heuristic, etc. However, connecting an MEIO application to SAP is actually fairly popular. I don't want to get into all the reasons why because the benefits are quite extensive, and I have a separate book that describes all of this, as well as an SCM Focus subsite focused exclusively on MEIO.

http://www.scmfocus.com/inventoryoptimizationmultiechelon/

Instead I will just focus on "how" to use MEIO in conjunction with SNP.

Using SNP with MEIO

MEIO applications can be used just as one would use any other supply planning application, and in this case the MEIO applications would replace SNP and send recommendations (stock transport requisitions, purchase requisitions) over to the ERP system. However, in the majority of cases, MEIO applications have been implemented as master data parameter generators.

MEIO Data Flow

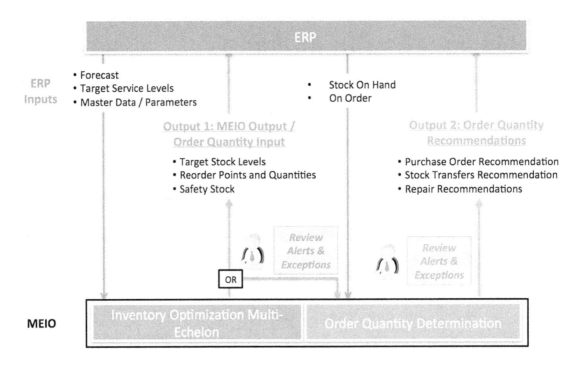

The above illustration is a simplified version of a graphic that was at one time used internally by MCA Solutions (now Servigistics). It shows the data flow into and out of an MEIO supply planning system. It also shows that a flow can be within the MEIO application, or can flow directly from the inventory and multi echelon optimization portion of the MEIO supply planning system to the ERP system. This is important, because some MEIO applications only produce and send Output 1, while other MEIO applications internally process Output 1, and it is not until Output 3 is generated that the output is sent to the ERP system. Companies that use the MEIO system for order quantity determination and supply planning benefit from a better interface and a more sophisticated planning system than is available in ERP. For companies that only use Output 1, the MEIO application more or less runs in the background. Planners require little training as they continue to use the ERP system for planning as they did prior to the MEIO implementation.

There are two common ways to connect MEIO to SAP, both to SAP SNP and to SAP ERP:

1. By passing planning recommendations (stock transfer requests, purchase requisitions)
2. Through updating parameters on either the product-location master (in APO) or the material master (in ERP)

When the first option is used, the MEIO application becomes the external planning system—in effect replacing SNP or being used in lieu of SNP. Therefore, I will not focus on the first option in this book as it does not combine MEIO with SNP.

When the second option is used, two things must occur in order for an MEIO application's output to be properly used by SNP or ERP. First, the actual values must come across from the MEIO application, and second, the options must be set properly to use these values.

Common parameters, which are updated, are the following:

1. *Safety Stock:* Here the safety stock key method is set to MB. When this occurs, safety stock is loaded as a key figure in the Planning Book.
2. *Target Stock Level:* The quantity that the SNP heuristic should plan that product location for.
3. *Max Stock Level:* The quantity SNP should never exceed.

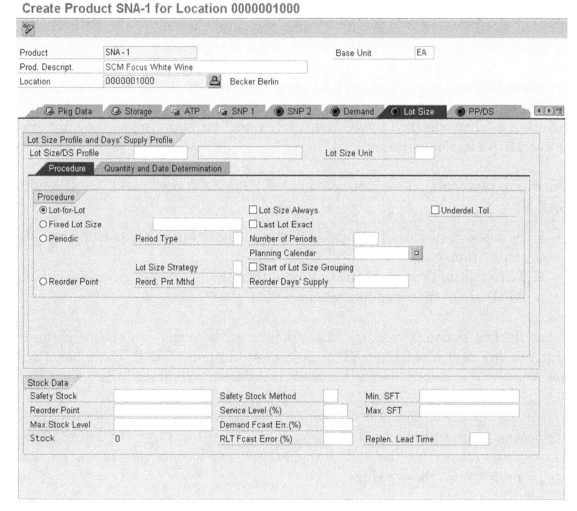

All of the input parameters discussed above are on the lot size tab in the product-location master.

Using the Different Master Data Parameters from the MEIO Application

While safety stock is probably the most commonly exported and used output from MEIO applications, of the three different methods, using the target stock level makes the greatest use of the MEIO application. In this scenario, the MEIO application is doing most of the heavy lifting, and SNP— through its heuristic—simply enforces the target stock level, which is calculated with the MEIO application's more sophisticated mathematics.

A company can choose to populate one, two or all three of the parameters with the MEIO application. The values that are calculated by the MEIO application should be both lower and more accurate than the values calculated by other means. MEIO can see all of the location relationships in the entire supply network and provide output that is considerate of the "bigger picture" of the overall stocking levels.

The Human and Process Challenges of Combining MEIO and Other Supply Planning Applications

Most of the literature about integrating MEIO applications with other supply planning applications focuses on the technical aspects of integration. However, when integrating MEIO through master data parameters (or "modifiers"), the technical challenges are actually not nearly as great as assumed. The much larger issue is the process integration that is required, but so often underemphasized on these types of projects. At several clients, I have witnessed the MEIO input improperly used because of how the MEIO output was integrated from a process perspective. For instance, at one client MEIO output was brought into SNP, however, the management at the company insisted on keeping the same target days' supply levels that they had been using for years, prior to the MEIO software being integrated with SNP. MEIO will calculate lower safety stock and target stock levels or maximum stock levels than would be calculated without the advanced mathematics of MEIO. This is because MEIO is the one supply planning method that can interpret planned inventory levels based upon the inventory levels at connected locations. This concept of effective lead time is explained in the link below:

http://www.scmfocus.com/inventoryoptimizationmultiechelon/2010/01/ effective-lead-time-and-multi-echelon/

In my opinion, the reason that management kept the pre-MEIO target days' supply in SNP is that MEIO was never effectively socialized, and therefore, they did not trust its planning output. The lack of solution socialization turns out to be the Achilles heel in the implementation of all of the more complex methods, not only supply planning software but supply chain planning software generally. Furthermore, in over fifteen years of working on advanced planning implementations, I have not seen solution socialization improve one bit. In fact, it may even be worse now than when these more advanced methods were first introduced. Aside from relatively light articles on the importance of "change management," few concrete steps are taken to improve this socialization, particularly by the major consulting companies. However, how to effectively socialize complex solutions is no great mystery, but it does require adjustments to the business-as-usual approach to software implementation. How to properly socialize optimization software is discussed at the link below:

http://www.scmfocus.com/inventoryoptimizationmultiechelon/2011/05/
socializing-supply-chain-optimization/

Conclusion

This chapter is different from the other chapters in this book because it describes how to incorporate a different method, which is outside of APO but used by APO (or SAP ERP). The MEIO supply planning method is the most popular external supply planning method to integrate with SNP. The most frequently used parameters that are exported from MEIO systems to either SNP or to ERP are the safety stock, target stock level, and max stock level, with the target stock level being the modifier which has the strongest influence over the supply plan.

While the technical implementation of MEIO is challenging, the integration of the MEIO output to a system like SNP is not particularly challenging. It turns out that one of the biggest challenges to MEIO implementations in terms of integrating the MEIO output into the legacy planning system from a process perspective has been the human element. There is simply no way around socializing the MEIO solution.

CHAPTER 11

Conclusion

Implementing a multi method approach requires more thought and a few more configuration adjustments than a single method approach; however, a multi method approach does a better job of meeting business requirements and of allowing a company to use a single external planning environment, which has many associated benefits. The common business requirement of using multiple supply planning methods is often achieved by splitting the product-location database between the ERP system and the external planning system. However, it is increasingly more common for companies to plan all products in the external planning system, which also happens to be the direction at SAP.

It is quite feasible to combine multiple supply planning methods and method modifiers in SAP SNP, as well as in a number of other supply planning applications. What are missing is both the publications to show how this is accomplished and the consultants who are experienced and primed to help walk companies through the necessary explanation, configuration and prototyping.

The various supply planning alternatives presented in this book are a combination of the methods, along with method modifiers. Some method modifiers only work with some methods, and explaining this to the business decision makers so they can decide which method and method modifiers to use is an important part of the implementation process. While a company that moves to an external planning system will use a new method, many of the method modifiers may be same as those they currently use. There is every reason to leverage the modifiers that the company has been using for years in their ERP system.

The common rule of thumb regarding the necessity of dividing the product-location database between the ERP system and the external planning system is dated and is based upon hardware limitations that no longer apply. Perhaps we need to begin teaching the history of planning, because the field is suffering from a collective inability to record or recall its history. The conversation is generally controlled by the new pronouncements of software vendors. However, without some type of historical perspective, the ability to critically analyze either old rules of thumb or new concepts is greatly reduced.

One of the most important ways of improving a supply planning implementation—and improving the sustainability of the live solution—is by documenting both the configuration and the parameters in the product-location master. This documentation, part of which I have shown in screen shots of the demo map, is used to do everything from setting up the prototype to performing the final configuration.

Prototyping is critical to successful planning software implementations. A prototype shows business decision makers how the system works; this is important, as doing so enables them to make decisions about how to set up the project. Many consulting companies prefer to skip prototyping so they can spoon feed significant business decisions to their clients and extend out implementations as long as possible. This large consulting company model is based upon maximizing billing hours, and is not part of good implementation practice. If a project's timelines are such that there is "not time for prototyping," then the project has not been set up correctly, and the company needs to re-evaluate its project plan and budget, and possibly its scope.

This book demonstrated a three-test prototype, which showed that multiple supply planning methods can be used in conjunction and without issue and also provided an example of how to properly document the results of a prototype test.

The three prototype tests performed in Chapter 5: "Prototyping the Multi Method Supply Planning Model" used one method per echelon in the supply network. In real life, there will be different methods and method modifiers run for at least some of the echelons. This requirement can be easily met by always processing the supply network from "top to bottom" and in sequence, such that the distribution centers are processed first, and then the regional distribution centers, and then the finished goods factory, and so on. This rule of thumb works well because the interaction between locations is vertical and not horizontal during the initial supply plan and during the deployment (although not during the redeployment planning run). Processing the supply network echelon by echelon enforces the vertical flow through the supply network.

Understanding how to set up the dynamic master data selection for all the methods in SNP is an important foundational configuration approach for creating a lower maintenance design for implementing a multi method supply planning approach. These steps are outlined in this book.

Outside of books on project management or change management, the human aspect of system implementation is not frequently discussed, even though it is as important as any other aspect of implementation. The shortage of consultants who are familiar with the multi method approach, as well as the shortage of publications on this topic, are examples of the human aspect that can prevent the effective implementation of the multi-method approach. There are valid concerns with regard to the multi-method approach. However, a multi-method approach can also be opposed to simply because the consultants cannot "wrap their heads around" how to make the approach work. That is the main point of this book: to not only describe the benefits of the multi-method approach, but to show specifically how the approach can be set up in SNP.

MEIO does not exist in SNP, but it is common to combine an MEIO application with SNP. While the rest of the book describes how to set up multiple methods within SNP, this chapter differs in that it focuses on the MEIO method, which can only be incorporated into SNP by integrating to another application. MEIO implementations can be challenging, but from my observation of a number of projects where both SNP and an MEIO application were co-implemented, I have found that one of the biggest challenges is simply to understand how SNP should use the output of the MEIO application from a process perspective.

In summary, there are many opportunities to use multiple supply planning methods in SNP, as well as bringing in the output of non-SNP supply planning methods—such as MEIO—into SNP. The multi-method approach to supply planning enables companies to meet the common business requirement, and to do so in one external planning system. This book has explained how to accomplish the multi supply planning method approach in SNP, but it can similarly be accomplished in other supply planning applications.

Links in the Book

Chapter 1

http://www.scmfocus.com/sapprojectmanagement/2010/07/how-valid-are-saps-best-practice-claims/

http://www.scmfocus.com/enterprisesoftwarepolicy/2012/03/08/how-lying-is-an-advantage-in-the-enterprise-software-market/

http://www.scmfocus.com/writing-rules/

http://www.scmfocus.com

http://www.scmfocus.com/supplyplanning.

http://www.scmfocus.com/sapplanning.

Chapter 2

http://www.scmfocus.com/supplyplanning/2011/10/02/the-four-factors-that-make-up-the-master-production-schedule/

http://www.scmfocus.com/inventoryoptimizationmultiechelon/2011/10/redeployment/

http://www.scmfocus.com/sapplanning/2008/09/14/resources/

http://www.scmfocus.com/sapplanning/2009/12/08/customer-prioritization-and-ctm/

http://www.scmfocus.com/sapplanning/2012/10/07/forecast-based-forward-calculating-reorder-points/

http://www.scmfocus.com/demandplanning/2010/07/using-demandworks-smoothie-for-forecast-prototyping/

http://www.scmfocus.com/demandplanning/2012/02/combining-the-hierarchies-of-two-different-demand-planning-systems/

http://www.scmfocus.com/sapplanning/2012/07/24/synchronizing-integrated-factories-with-stock-transfers/

http://www.scmfocus.com/demandplanning/2012/03/how-trader-joes-reduces-lumpy-demand/

http://www.scmfocus.com/sapplanning/2009/05/09/ctm/

http://www.scmfocus.com/sapplanning/2009/12/08/customer-prioritization-and-ctm/

http://www.scmfocus.com/sapprojectmanagement/2010/07/how-valid-are-saps-best-practice-claims/

http://www.scmfocus.com/supplyplanning/2011/10/02/commonly-used-and-unused-constraints-for-supply-planning/

http://www.scmfocus.com/supplychaininnovation/2010/08/the-benefit-of-blended-solutions-based-upon-component-based-software/

http://www.scmfocus.com/demandplanning/2010/07/using-demandworks-smoothie-for-forecast-prototyping/

http://www.scmfocus.com/demandplanning/2012/02/combining-the-hierarchies-of-two-different-demand-planning-systems/

Chapter 3

http://www.scmfocus.com/sapplanning/2009/05/15/sap-scm-vs-apo/

http://www.scmfocus.com/demandplanning/2012/03/why-not-all-attribute-and-rolap-solutions-are-equal/

http://www.scmfocus.com/scmfocuspress/select-a-book/the-software-approaches-for-improving-your-bill-of-materials-book/

http://www.scmfocus.com/supplyplanning/2011/06/27/product-database-segmentation-between-erp-and-external-supply-planning-systems/

http://www.scmfocus.com/scmbusinessintelligence/2011/07/the-amazing-disappearing-bi-reports/

Chapter 4

http://www.scmfocus.com/inventoryoptimizationmultiechelon/2011/05/socializing-supply-chain-optimization/

http://www.scmfocus.com/sapplanning/2009/11/08/scm-simulation-archival-blog/

http://www.scmfocus.com/demandplanning/2010/06/forecastable-non-forecastable-formula/

http://www.scmfocus.com/sapplanning/2011/06/09/the-planning-book-key-figure-and-macro-definitions/

http://www.scmfocus.com/sapplanning/2010/02/24/the-storage-buckets-profile-and-the-planning-buckets-profile/

http://www.scmfocus.com/sapplanning/2011/02/17/creating-telescoping-view-in-the-planning-book/

http://www.scmfocus.com/sapplanning/2011/06/09/order-and-forecast-categories/

Chapter 5

http://www.scmfocus.com/supplychainsimulation/2012/05/27/mrp-drp-prototyping-external-systems/

http://www.scmfocus.com/sapprojectmanagement/2010/06/what-percentage-of-the-hourly-rate-is-taken-by-the-partner/

http://www.scmfocus.com/sapprojectmanagement/2012/02/deloittes-puffery-in-their-rfp-to-marin-county-and-what-it-means-for-current-and-future-clients/

http://www.scmfocus.com/sapprojectmanagement/2012/02/has-deloitte-bought-off-someone-inside-your-organization-as-they-did-with-marin-county/

http://www.scmfocus.com/sapplanning/2011/10/12/using-an-external-system-to-check-optimization-results/

http://www.scmfocus.com/demandplanning/2010/07/prototype-environment-and-background/

http://www.scmfocus.com/sapplanning/2008/09/14/quota-arrangements-in-scm/

http://www.scmfocus.com/sapplanning/2011/12/20/running-the-optimizer-for-a-single-location-versus-the-sub-problem/

http://www.scmfocus.com/sapplanning/2012/06/19/should-ctm-be-run-daily-or-interactively/

Chapter 6

http://www.scmfocus.com/supplychainmasterdata/2011/05/methodology-for-adjusting-master-data/

http://www.scmfocus.com/supplychainmasterdata/2010/06/why-software-based-mdm-is-a-consulting-boondoggle/

http://www.scmfocus.com/enterprisesoftwarepolicy/2011/11/29/how-efficient-is-the-market-for-enterprise-software/

Chapter 7

http://www.scmfocus.com/inventoryoptimizationmultiechelon/2011/10/redeployment/

Chapter 9

http://www.scmfocus.com/inventoryoptimizationmultiechelon/2010/10/booz-allen-hamilton-misrepresents-inventory-optimization-in-white-papers/

http://www.scmfocus.com/demandplanning/2012/02/how-much-can-your-forecasting-accuracy-be-improved/

http://www.scmfocus.com/demandplanning/2012/03/how-trader-joes-reduces-lumpy-demand/

http://www.scmfocus.com/demandplanning/2010/09/why-companies-are-selecting-the-wrong-supply-chain-demand-planning-systems/

http//www.scmfocus.com/consulting/why-big-consulting-firms-cannot-do-software-selection/

http://www.scmfocus.com/demandplanning/2012/01/demand-shaping-and-demand-sensing/

http://www.scmfocus.com/demandplanning/2012/03/outsourced-forecasting/

http://www.scmfocus.com/sapprojectmanagement/2010/06/the-role-of-the-business-lead/

http://www.scmfocus.com/sapprojectmanagement/2011/07/the-ibm-systems-implementation-approach/

http://www.scmfocus.com/sapplanning/2011/02/04/level-of-bom-planning-in-the-snp-heuristic-and-low-level-codes/

Chapter 10

http://www.scmfocus.com/inventoryoptimizationmultiechelon/

http://www.scmfocus.com/inventoryoptimizationmultiechelon/2010/01/effective-lead-time-and-multi-echelon/

http://www.scmfocus.com/inventoryoptimizationmultiechelon/2011/05/socializing-supply-chain-optimization/

References

Capacity Planning in Repetitive Manufacturing. SAP AG, 2001.
http://help.sap.com/printdocu/core/Print46c/en/data/pdf/PPCRPREM/
PPCRP_REM.pdf

Clark, A.J. *A Dynamic Single-Item, Multi Echelon Inventory Model.*
RAND Corporation, 1958.

Conversion of SNP and CTM Orders into PP/DS Orders.
http://help.sap.com/saphelp_em70/helpdata/en/c5/c4703736bfb37de
10000009b38f8cf/content.htm

Creating SNP Planned Orders from SAP R/3.
http://help.sap.com/saphelp_scm50/helpdata/en/b3/32c5d32970834
dadf53cac0aa2b5b4/content.htm

*Have weather forecasts improved in accuracy over the last 50
years? Last* modified October 13, 2010. http://www.quora.com/
Have-weather-forecasts-improved-in-accuracy-over-the-last-50-years

Integrating SNP and PP/DS
http://help.sap.com/saphelp_em70/helpdata/en/f1/c2d837ffbf2424e
10000009b38f889/content.htm

Integration of Purchase Orders and Purchase Requisitions.
http://help.sap.com/saphelp_scm50/helpdata/en/01/0d9d18a91011
d5b4750050dadf0791/content.htm

Mass Production. Last modified December 13, 2012.
http://en.wikipedia.org/wiki/Mass_production

Mass Production. Last modified December 15, 2012.
http://en.wikipedia.org/wiki/Prototype

Mass Production. Last modified November 30, 2012.
http://en.wikipedia.org/wiki/Instructions_per_second

Manage Supply Network Planning in CTM in SAP APO, SAP. November, 2008.

Sales and Invetory Planning with SAP APO (excerpt). SAP Press, 2007.
http://www.sap-press.de/katalog/buecher/htmlleseproben/gp/htmlprobID-146

Snapp, Shaun. *Planning System Timings.* Last modified February 17, 2010.
http://www.scmfocus.com/sapplanning/2010/02/17/planning-cadence/

Thonta, Srini. *SAP APO Global ATP.* 2008.
http://www.cogentibs.com/pdf/cogsap08/GATP.pdf

Vendor Acknowledgements and Profiles

Below are brief profiles of each vendor for which I included screen shots in this book.

Profiles:

SAP

SAP does not need much of an introduction. They are the largest vendor of enterprise software applications for supply chain management. SAP has multiple products that are showcased in this book, including SAP ERP and SAP SCM/APO SNP and SAP SCM/APO SPP.

www.sap.com

Barloworld

Barloworld has 350 customers for its supply chain planning and network planning tools, covering such industries as automotive, industrial, retail, wholesale and distribution. The supply chain planning product set offers a focused supply chain planning footprint.

www.barloworld.com

Demand Works

Demand Works is a best-of-breed demand and supply planning vendor that emphasizes flexible and easy-to-configure solutions. This book only focuses on the supply planning functionality within their Smoothie product, which includes MRP and DRP.

www.demandworks.com

Author Profile

Shaun Snapp is the Founder and Editor of SCM Focus. SCM Focus is one of the largest independent supply chain software analysis and educational sites on the Internet.

After working at several of the largest consulting companies and at i2 Technologies, he became an independent consultant and later started SCM Focus. He maintains a strong interest in comparative software design, and works both in SAP APO, as well as with a variety of best-of-breed supply chain planning vendors. His ongoing relationships with these vendors keep him on the cutting edge of emerging technology.

Primary Sources of Information and Writing Topics

Shaun writes about topics with which he has first-hand experience. These topics range from recovering problematic implementations, to system configuration, to socializing complex software and supply chain concepts in the areas of demand planning, supply planning and production planning.

More broadly, he writes on topics supportive of these applications, which include master data parameter management, integration, analytics, simulation and bill of material management systems. He covers management aspects of enterprise software ranging from software policy to handling consulting partners on SAP projects.

Shaun writes from an implementer's perspective and as a result he focuses on how software is actually used in practice rather than its hypothetical or "pure release note capabilities." Unlike many authors in enterprise software who keep their distance from discussing the realities of software implementation, he writes both on the problems as well as the successes of his software use. This gives him a distinctive voice in the field.

Secondary Sources of Information
In addition to project experience, Shaun's interest in academic literature is a secondary source of information for his books and articles. Intrigued with the historical perspective of supply chain software, much of his writing is influenced by his readings and research into how different categories of supply chain software developed, evolved, and finally became broadly used over time.

Covering the Latest Software Developments
Shaun is focused on supply chain software selections and implementation improvement through writing and consulting, bringing companies some of the newest technologies and methods. Some of the software developments that Shaun showcases at SCM Focus and in books at SCM Focus Press have yet to reach widespread adoption.

Education
Shaun has an undergraduate degree in business from the University of Hawaii, a Masters of Science in Maritime Management from the Maine Maritime Academy and a Masters of Science in Business Logistics from Penn State University. He has taught both logistics and SAP software.

Software Certifications
Shaun has been trained and/or certified in products from i2 Technologies, Servigistics, ToolsGroup and SAP (SD, DP, SNP, SPP, EWM).

Contact
Shaun can be contacted at: shaunsnapp@scmfocus.com www.scmfocus.com/

Abbreviations

(SAP) APO – Advanced Planning and Optimizer

APS – Advanced Planning and Scheduling

BAPI – Business Application Programming Interface

(SAP) BW – Business Warehouse

BOM – Bill of Material

(SAP) CTM – Capable to Match

DC – Distribution Center

(SAP) DP – Demand Planner

(SAP) GATP – Global Available to Promise

RDC – Regional Distribution Center

DRP – Distribution Resource Planning

ERP – Enterprise Resource Planning

MASSD – Not an acronym, but the mass maintenance transaction in SAP APO.

(SAP) MDG – Master Data Governance

MDM – Master Data Management

MEIO – Inventory Optimization and Multi echelon Planning

MPS – Master Production Schedule

MRP – Materials Requirements Planning

(SAP) PP/DS – Production Planning and Detailed Scheduling

RDC – Regional Distribution Center

ROLAP - Relational On Line Analytical Processing

SAPGUI – SAP Graphical User Interface

(SAP) SCE – Supply Chain Engineer

(SAP) SNP – Supply Network Planning

S&OP – Sales and Operations Planning

STO – Stock Transport Order

STR – Stock Transport Requisition

SYSID – System Identifier

TDS – Target Days' Supply

TSL – Target Stock Level (is also the acronym for "Target Service Level." Interestingly in MEIO software the Target Stock Level is based upon the Target Service Level—leading to more acronym confusion. But in this book, TSL is the Target Stock Level).